"We all need aids on our way to God and with God. The authors make a compelling case that art can be such an aid and then show how. Anne Bent's meditations and prayers exude attentive admiration for art and authentic devotion to God."

—MIROSLAV VOLF,
professor of theology, Yale University and co-author of *Life Worth Living: A Guide to What Matters Most* (2023).

"A fascinating mixture of art, spirituality, and theology, as an expert theologian and artist collaborate to take us on a rich journey through various Old Master drawings of biblical and spiritual themes, sensitively explained and each concluding with helpful meditations and prayers to assist us to discover art as a 'Way to God.'"

—RICHARD A. BURRIDGE,
professor of theology,
University of Manchester

"Art aficionado Anne Bent and Christian thought leader Ian Markham have given us food for eyes, mind, and heart. We are shown how to think theologically about art and inducted into a new journey with God. A gift both for spiritual seekers and Christians facing the long haul, *Art and the Experience of the Divine* helps us to see, to pray, and to give thanks."

—SCOTT COWDELL,
research professor in theology,
Charles Sturt University

"The rich and ancient relationship between religious experience and beliefs and art is a fascinating topic to explore. The approach of the authors (a Christian theologian and an expert in Old Master Drawings) is fresh, informal, and invitational. The authors invite the reader to think with them in an informed and interdisciplinary way, about how art can and does inform and enrich religious beliefs and feelings, and in turn, how religious beliefs and feelings help shape one's perceptions of works of art."

—HEIDI HADSELL,

president emeritus,

Hartford International University of Religion and Peace

Art *and the* Experience *of the* Divine

Art *and the* Experience *of the* Divine

Anne Searle Bent
&
Ian S. Markham

WIPF & STOCK · Eugene, Oregon

ART AND THE EXPERIENCE OF THE DIVINE

Wipf and Stock Publishers
199 W. 8th Ave., Suite 3
Eugene, OR 97401

www.wipfandstock.com

PAPERBACK ISBN: 978-1-6667-7572-3
HARDCOVER ISBN: 978-1-6667-7573-0
EBOOK ISBN: 978-1-6667-7574-7

Cataloguing-in-Publication data:

Names: Bent, Anne Searle [author]. | Markham, Ian S. [author].

Title: Art and the experience of the Divine / Anne Searle Bent and Ian S. Markham.

Description: Eugene, OR: Wipf and Stock Publishers, 2024 | Includes bibliographical references.

Identifiers: ISBN 978-1-6667-7572-3 (paperback) | ISBN 978-1-6667-7573-0 (hardcover) | ISBN 978-1-6667-7574-7 (ebook)

Subjects: LCSH: Christian art and symbolism. | Christianity and art. | Spirituality in art. | Spiritual life—Christianity. | Spirituality. | Art and religion.

Classification: BV150 B46 2024 (paperback) | BV150 (ebook)

VERSION NUMBER 11/04/24

Saint Peter Liberated from Prison by Baccio Bandinelli

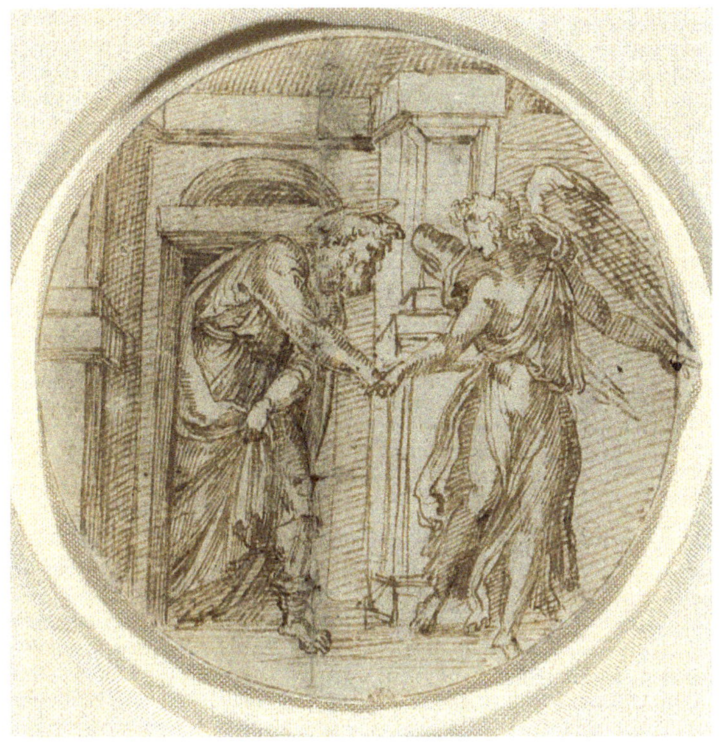

Contents

Acknowledgments

Together we want to acknowledge the gift of the Rev. Robin Parry of Wipf and Stock Publishers, who saw the potential in the project and supported it. Our research assistant, Ms. Elizabeth Clarke (known to us as Beth) played a crucial role in the concluding stages. We had a delightful day with the Rev. Luke Back and the Rev. Dr. Barney Hawkins, who read the manuscript closely and made numerous suggestions to improve the book.

FROM ANNE BENT

Ian was my professor before we became close friends. When I left VTS he encouraged me to "write my book." When we chose to work together, Ian took on a complete novice, brave man that he is. Ian is serious, hard working, and fun to boot. I am utterly grateful and completely devoted to him. Rev. Luke Back originally encouraged me to write about my old master drawings during the Covid era, which has changed my trajectory all for the best. The result of Luke's suggestion are the devotions herein. He has been a steadfast spiritual companion and good friend all along the way. Suzanne McCullagh read the manuscript and provided many helpful suggestions. Thomas Williams has provided encouragement and guidance through each part of this work. I am indebted to each of them.

Rev. Barney Hawkins was the first person I met at Virginia Theological Seminary. I've had the privilege of traveling with Barney to the Holy Land before Covid began. That was January of 2020. Barney is a man of deep abiding faith who quietly and steadily nurtured us, his flock, through that experience. Barney has the unique ability to bring out the God-sent aspect of those he cares for as fellow Christians on pilgrimage. I feel that "all things are possible" when I'm around him. It is a joy to have his encouragement in bringing this book to fruition.

My family has provided a willing ear, encouragement, and love throughout these past few years. While this arena, which Ian and I came into together, is new, both my husband Stephen and my children Marion and Ethan have been enthusiastic in their support, even if they are sometimes mystified by my fervor for it all. I love them and am very grateful to have each of them in my life. Finally, I thank God for all that God has so generously bestowed on me. My gratitude is boundless.

FROM IAN MARKHAM

Over several years, Anne has become a close friend. She has helped me appreciate the extraordinary world of "old master drawings." And when she intimated that she would like to collaborate on a book with me, I was delighted. We shared a conviction that art can be a powerful way to engage the heart in the encounter with God. I am deeply grateful to Anne.

I am also grateful to the numerous colleagues who understand that my passion for writing is an important part of my vocation. So thank you to Taryn Habberley, Melody Knowles, Jacqui Ballou, Linda Dienno, Lisa Kimball, Rachelle Sam, Nicky Burridge, and Michael DeLashmutt. My Board Chair, David Charlton, has been a model of presence and wisdom.

Finally, the journey of life is enhanced every single day by the presence of my wife Lesley and my son Luke. And it is a joy to have Sam Brooks, Luke's wife, joining the family. Thank you all for simply being wonderful.

CHAPTER ONE

Art as a Way to God

"I was born, one might say, between heaven and earth, that the world is for me a great desert in which my soul wanders like a torch, I did these paintings in unison with this distant dream."[1]

—Marc Chagall

Strangely, despite all the evidence to the contrary, we constantly imagine that humans are simply rational agents who are expected to consider everything through the lens of reason. Emotions and experiences are denigrated. We should be dispassionate and analytical. Logical arguments should be the control on our worldview.

Yet, this anthropology is too limited. We are not rational brains on legs. Instead, we are walking, talking, embodied people who love, laugh, fear, hate, and feel. Imagining that life is primarily a philosophy class where we need to find issues and evaluate those issues by using philosophical tools like logic and evidence ignores the reality of living. Thanks to psychology and sociology, we now know people are much more complex than that. Our subconscious is vast and deep. This is the realm where countless decisions are made. Our sexual needs, our cultural affiliations, and our sense of self are all in the non-rational realm. Consider the deep, powerful feeling of love: the love we have for those near to us transcends

1. Sotheby's, "Chagall."

reason. Our love for country and a willingness to die for that country transcend reason. Many of our deepest convictions are not subject to reason. Our sense that child abuse is abhorrent is not the result of an exercise in thinking and evaluation. It is almost spontaneous and deeply seated.

There is, of course, a place for reason. Reason is a key conversation partner. If we do not pause and subject our deepest desires to some rational critique and reflection, then there is a danger of letting the sins of prejudice run wild and of license being granted to patriarchy, homophobia, and racism. The right way to proceed, therefore, is for us to acknowledge that we are a result of social and psychological shaping that should be in conversation with the God-given gift of reason. Reason plays the important role of searching out irrational prejudice and fears, which can be so damaging to self and to others.

To be effective, the church needs to communicate to the non-rational sides of being human. We need to connect to the side of us that is the realm of love, patriotism, impulsive fears and hopes, and our sense of self in the world. Very few people (perhaps none) have been argued into faith. People are not persuaded by, for example, the "cosmological argument" for the existence of God. Intellectual assent that God is a possibility is not faith. Faith is when you feel God as a presence in your life.

The church believes in the spiritual realm. Naturalism (the view that only the material exists) is false. We are much more than just bundles of atoms. Our task in evangelism is to connect (or perhaps *re*connect, given that children seem to have an innate sense of God)[2] people to the spiritual realm. Reason is important; it is a God-given tool, but only a tool. It is one of many such tools. When I pray in an empty church, reason may say that the room is empty, but I say the chapel is full of the presence of God. All the traditional empirical tests of presence and absence will not work. Yet the experience is decisive. I finish my prayers knowing that I have been in the presence of God.

2. See Berryman, *Children*.

The two authors of this book believe that inviting others into the journey of faith is an invitation into the thin spaces where heaven meets earth. The painter Marc Chagall—Jewish by religion and passionate about the Bible—believed that his art was birthed in that space between heaven and earth. So perhaps artists are amongst those we should look to as companions on the way. Our own experience, and that of many others, is that the visual arts can indeed be a medium that connects us with God. As one studies the extraordinary creativity of an artist, one can be drawn to feel, indeed experience, the world in a different way. We believe that this can be your own experience too. With the aid of the meditation, you are invited to enjoy the great art and reflect on a theme that we hope and trust will bring you nearer to God.

The experience of this book is that the visual arts can be a medium that connects you—the reader—with God. As one studies the extraordinary creativity of an artist, one can be drawn to feel, indeed experience, the world in a different way. We are hoping for a dynamic experience—in which readers are shaped by the encounter of their own inner lives with both the art and the written meditative exploration of it—culminating in a sense of God.

The primary audience for this book is those seeking to grow into a deeper relationship with God. In Sikhism, there is that lovely saying: "When you walk one step towards God, God walks a thousand steps towards you."[3] Our hope is that our readers will take that one step towards God and then realize that God has taken the thousand steps towards them.

In addition, we have an agenda. We want a church where art in general and the visual arts in particular are part of our congregational life. We believe passionately that more art will result in more Christians. We want congregational leadership to invest in the arts and create art exhibits where people are invited to reflect on the spiritual. To this end, we have a substantial chapter that seeks to set out the relationship of theology to art and make the case that art can be an effective way into the divine.

3. See Khalsa, "Highest Meditation."

If you wish, dear reader, you can move from this chapter straight to chapter 3. It is there you will receive an introduction to the world of "old master drawings." Then you can move to enjoying the devotions. Chapter 2 is for those who want to explore in some detail the extraordinary world of theology and art. Why is it that art can be so important for the experience of faith? Much of the chapter is fairly technical. For those who need the theory to open up the devotions, then do explore the theology of art; but for those who simply want to start praying and experiencing God through the art, then you have our permission to move on to chapter 3.

CHAPTER TWO

Theology and Art

A VERITABLE INDUSTRY HAS emerged in recent years looking at theology and art. The literature comes from every conceivable vantage point: some have explored the use of religious imagery in art; others have focused on the artist as creator and drawn analogies with the creatorial work of God. Our focus is on the ways in which art can be revelatory of the God we worship and, within that, how art can show us God.

In Noel Carroll's exceptionally good introduction to the *Philosophy of Art*, he focuses on five primary theories of the nature of art.[1] The first theory is the neo-representation theory of art. It is called neo-representation theory because it is not simply imitation (art is just showing us what things are like); instead, art is more complex than that. Carroll explains:

> According to the neo-representational theory of art, anything that is a work of art necessarily possesses the property of aboutness—it has semantic content: it has a subject about which it expresses something: *King Lear*, for example, has a subject, governance, about which it says something: a house divided shall not stand. Likewise, Picasso's *Guernica* is about something, aerial bombardment, about which it expresses horror.[2]

1. Carroll, *Philosophy of Art*.
2. Carroll, *Philosophy of Art*, 27.

In other words, the goal of art is to say something about the world; it is, if you like, a complex mirror that is being held up to the world. On this view, there is a connection between the piece of art and the subject of the art, which is part of the world.

The problem with seeing art as a representation or resemblance of things in the world is that both photography and science do a better job at explaining how the world is. So, a second theory of art emerged. This is the expression theory of art. Art is best understood as sharing the inner turmoil of the artist—the soul is being exposed in the piece of art. Carroll writes:

> An important example of this seismic shift in artistic ambition was the Romantic movement. In 1798, in the Preface to his *Lyrical Ballads,* Wordsworth maintains that poetry "is the spontaneous overflow of powerful feelings." That is, the role of the poet is not essentially to mirror the action of other people, but to explore his or her own feelings. Romanticism places premier value on the self and its own individual experiences. Where the poet contemplates some outward scene, the scene is not presented for its own sake, but as a stimulus for the poet to examine his or her own emotional responses to it.[3]

On this view, unlike the first theory where art is a mirror reflecting the world, this time art is a mirror reflecting the self.

The third theory of art is a result of more abstract works of art emerging. Photography is the best instrument for actually capturing the world. So, abstract art focuses on form. This becomes art as formalism. When it comes to cubism and minimalism, we are not seeking to represent the world. Instead, explains Carroll, "Their aim was not to capture the perceptual appearances of the world, but often to make images noteworthy for their visual organization, form, and arresting design."[4] It was Clive Bell who became the leading exponent of this theory of art. For Bell, significant form is what determines whether a painting is art—form in terms of

3. Carroll, *Philosophy of Art*, 59.

4. Carroll, *Philosophy of Art*, 108.

the "arrangement of lines, colors, shapes, volumes, vectors, and space."[5]

The fourth theory focuses on aesthetics. It is interesting to note that the *viewer* of the art has not been prominent in theories two and three—two with the focus on the *artist* and three with the focus on the achievement of *form*. The aesthetic theory of art focuses on "the audience's portion of the interaction between artworks and readers, listeners and viewers."[6] For the aesthetic theorist of art, "there is something special about our commerce with artworks. Artworks, she claims, affords a unique kind of experience. The experiences we have strolling through a gallery or seated in a concert hall are different in kind from other sorts of experience like completing tax forms, shoveling snow, buying groceries, building rocket ships, or writing new bulletins."[7] On this view, the hope is that one arrives at a contemplative state. The goal of art is to provoke aesthetic experiences.

The fifth theory of art is inspired by theorist Ludwig Wittgenstein. Wittgenstein took the view that searching for a single definition of art was impossible. There are not a set of qualities that all forms of art share. Instead, similar to the way in which members in a family can share certain overlapping features, even though no single feature (such as blue eyes) characterizes all of them, so "art" is a word that covers a range of diverse kinds of work, including music, drawing, and sculpture, which have no single core thing in common but which do have a range of overlapping qualities and resemblances.

Carroll has provided a helpful taxonomy that illuminates the complex relationship between the world, the artist, the viewer, and the actual piece of art, especially its form. However, the taxonomy is completely secular. It works on the assumption that the experience of art is entirely understood in the human realm. We wish to make the claim that art engages the spiritual realm, thus we need a sixth theory of art that emphasizes the spiritual.

5. Carroll, *Philosophy of Art*, 109.

6. Carroll, *Philosophy of Art*, 157.

7. Carroll, *Philosophy of Art*, 160.

THE SPIRITUAL THEORY OF ART

There are two reasons why this is important. First, many pieces of art are inspired by a religious impulse and often are about a religious topic. In the world of Islamic art, for example, there is a metaphysic underpinning the art. The scholar Seyyed Hossein Nasr is harsh on those who seek to interpret Islamic art primarily through a socio-political lens. Instead, in Islamic metaphysics and theology, God is the source of art. Nasr writes, "The sacred art of Islam is, like all veritable sacred art, a descent of heavenly reality upon the earth. It is the crystallization of the spirit and form of the Islamic revelation dressed in the robe of a perfection which is not of this world of corruption and death. It is an echo of the other world (*al akhirah*) in the matrix of the temporal existence in which men live (*al dunya*)."[8] Islamic art is a connection between eternity and the present on earth. Within the Christian tradition, any study of the Renaissance authors reflecting on the artistic endeavor discovers that there is not only a deep religious practice underpinning the process but also an expectation of some form of disclosure of God to the viewer. So, in Cennino Cennini's handbook on painting, the author always invokes Christ and the Virgin before beginning his work; the art arrives at a point where the spiritual theme is communicated in such a way as to transcend the limitations of regular language.[9]

The second reason is that there is an entire tradition in art that frames the task in a spiritual way. It was the Russian painter Wassily Kandinsky in his book *Concerning the Spiritual in Art* who argued that the spiritual is a primary category in understanding art. Kandinsky was influenced by theosophy and spiritualism; he believed that artists needed to move beyond the traditional, learned skills—such as how to observe and paint—and to see their art as a mechanism to facilitate their spiritual growth. Mimi Farrelly-Hansen explains: "Having developed their own souls to the point of directly intuiting the spiritual dimension, artists must

8. Nasr, *Islamic Art*, 4.

9. See Stowell, *Spiritual Language of Art*.

express that larger metaphysical reality via subtle manipulations of non-objective form and color harmonies whose vibrations evoked a soul response in the viewer."[10] Kandinsky made many followers: Malevich, Marc, Klee, and Brancusi. They all saw art as this two-stage process: the growth of the soul of the artist to the point of union with universal Spirit and then, the second stage, the creation of art that evokes a spiritual insight in the viewer. This approach meant the definition of art was more inclusive. Kandinsky celebrated folk and primitive art, art by children, Asian and African art, and, importantly, the art created by those with mental illness.

Although some in this tradition might want to insist that all art must have this spiritual dimension, this is not our position. Wittgenstein here is helpful. The term art can and should extend beyond any particular invocation of experience. However, we do want to claim that the spiritual theory of art is an important feature of many forms of art (especially those seeking to stimulate religious reflection).

And this is not confined just to religious themed art. As C. Spretnak complains:

> Why is it that the millions of people in this country who have taken art history courses or attended museum exhibitions or collected books on a few favorite artists have most likely never encountered such basic information as the following? Mondrian's hard-edged grid paintings, considered by many to be the epitome of tough-minded modern art, were created to be modern visual expressions of the esoteric spiritual teachings of Theosophy. The reason Renoir loved to paint women, especially women in gardens, was that he considered the female face and body, along with nature, to be God's finest creation.[11]

Spretnak's point is well made. The spiritual theory of art is a necessary part of the understanding of many forms of art, not just the explicitly religious. There are some theologians who have wanted

10. Farrelly-Hansen, *Spirituality and Art Therapy*.

11. Spretnak, *Spiritual Dynamic*, 1.

to explicate the spiritual theory of art. It is to those voices that we turn next.

THEOLOGIANS AND ART

There are many substantial discussions of art by theologians. Indeed, a case could be made that almost all substantial theologians have some "theory of art." So, to make this manageable, I propose to focus on certain key thinkers who are representative of the field.

We start with Jacques Maritain. Maritain was a Roman Catholic philosopher who lived in France in the early to mid-twentieth century. He was part of the revival of interest in Thomas Aquinas and uses Aquinas in his critique of art.[12] For Maritain, art should not be judged by a moral frame. Indeed, Maritain quotes that lovely line from Oscar Wilde: "The fact of a man being a poisoner is nothing against his prose."[13] In other words, art is to do with beauty, but beauty need not emerge from a person of deep moral virtue. You can be a saint and a dreadful painter; you can also be villain and an extraordinary painter. The goal of art is beauty. Theologian Rowan Williams summarizes Maritain thus: "Beauty, we might paraphrase, is a relation between work and observer in which the observer's will as well as intellect is engaged, a relation in which what is present to the mind is sensed as desirable, as a source of pleasure."[14] However, although beauty is part of the task, this beauty needs to combine with integrity. In this sense, art is intellectual. Herein, the artist is making a claim about reality: art is orientated towards being (the way things really are in God). Maritain actually says of poetry that it is ontology, and what is true of poetry would also be true of the visual arts.[15] For Maritain, the precise relationship between art and ontology is complex. It is always partial; it is always incomplete. Williams summarizes thus: "The

12. See Williams, *Grace and Necessity.*
13. Maritain, *Art and Scholasticism*, 150.
14. Williams, *Grace and Necessity*, 12.
15. Williams, *Grace and Necessity*, 16.

mature Maritain, in the Mellon Lectures, speaks of finite beauty or finishedness in the work being always incomplete at some level, 'limping,' like the biblical Jacob, from the encounter with what cannot be named; achieved art always has 'that kind of imperfection through which infinity wounds the finite.'"[16]

In summary, then, we have the following picture of art in Maritain. The quest is beauty, which needs to be grounded in integrity. It is an action of the intelligence and therefore is making a claim about reality. The way it does this is by creating a way of seeing the world that is suggestive of the "beyond" (what we are calling the spiritual realm), which, of necessity, will be incomplete.

Turning now to George Steiner,[17] the great scholar of literature who worked at the Universities of Geneva, Oxford, Harvard, and Cambridge. Steiner argued for a necessary transcendental underpinning in all great art. In his famous book *Real Presences*, he argues, "The experience of aesthetic meaning in particular, that of literature, of the arts, of musical form, infers the necessary possibility of this 'real presence.'"[18] By real presence, Steiner means the transcendent. Steiner stresses two aspects of the aesthetic experience: the first is the depths to which a piece of music or a famous work of art can reach. Steiner writes, "Entering into us, the painting, the sonata, the poem brings us into reach of our nativity of consciousness. It does so at a depth inaccessible in any other way."[19] Granted, this experience of art needs cultivation and for this reason Steiner was a firm advocate for the education of children in the arts. The second aspect is that the act of creating great art is made possible because we ourselves are all creations.

Steiner is drawing attention to the genius that has the capacity to create *King Lear* or paint the *Mona Lisa*. Steiner writes:

> I can only put it this way (and every true poem, piece of music or painting says it better): there is aesthetic creation because there is creation. . . . I take the aesthetic

16. Williams, *Grace and Necessity*, 21.
17. See Markham, *Understanding Christian Doctrine*, 41–47.
18. Steiner, *Real Presences*, 3.
19. Steiner, *Real Presences*, 182.

> act, the conceiving and bringing into being of that which, very precisely, could not have been conceived or brought into being, to be an *imitatio*, a replication on its own scale, of the inaccessible first *fiat* (the "Big Bang" of the new cosmologies, before which there cannot be, in true Augustinian fashion, any "time," is no less a construed imperative and "boundary-condition" than is the narrative of creation in religion).[20]

The point is this: the miracle of great art or great music (the capacity to create inspirational and moving images or music from "nothing") is a human echo of the divine achievement of creating the cosmos out of nothing. For Steiner, great art is born of faith; it witnesses to faith.

Naturally, there are theologians who stress art as both revelatory of culture and art as a model for the work of the theologian. The two theologians best representing this approach are Paul Tillich and his disciple Gordon Kaufman. Paul Tillich sees art as descriptive of culture. In his *The System of the Sciences According to Object and Methods*, Tillich suggests there are three key steps in the religious analysis of art. The first step is the general religious analysis of art: this is where one learns from art about the state of culture. The second step is the religious history of art, which is where we listen to the art in culture and seek to discern religious themes in the art, even if the art is not ostensibly religious. And the third step is the "concrete religious systematization of art," which is where we seek to understand the emerging theology of the culture.[21] For Tillich, the primary emphasis in his critique of art is what we learn about a culture's religious discernment from art.

Meanwhile, Gordon Kaufman develops his own distinctive approach in his book *An Essay on Theological Method*.[22] For Kaufman, art is a creative enterprise as is theology. He stresses the parallels between artistic composition and theological composition as he sees it. For Kaufman, the artist uses imagination for a

20. Steiner, *Real Presences*, 201.

21. See Manning, "Towards a Critical Reconstruction," 32–37.

22. See Kaufman, *Theological Method*; Gunn, "On the Relation," 87–91.

constructive enterprise, and the criterion for an acceptable theology is in part controlled by aesthetic considerations (he thinks of a good theology as one that is beautiful in the sense that it is orientated to a just vision of the world). He thinks that this account of the parallels partly explains why art and theology constantly influence each other in history. Giles Gunn in his helpful article explains: "Theology has always relied on the testimony of artists, story-tellers, and bards to develop its imaginative conceptions of the world and of God. Conversely, art and literature have been deeply influenced by the critical and interpretive shapings and reshapings given by theologians to many of the most determinative images and metaphors in Western culture."[23]

Finally, we will consider Tongshik Ryu. Ryu is a leading Korean theologian who argues for a concept called *Pungryu*.[24] For Ryu, the "Asian" worldview places more emphasis on aesthetics than on argument. And the concept of *Pungryu* stresses "the 'religio-aesthetic' spirituality of one beautiful life in the Korean culture."[25] The result is a stress on beauty, on oneness, and on life. In this respect, art is therefore central. Ryu argues that beauty belongs to eternity, while the precise form that it will take belongs to time and space. Given this, art then becomes a bridge, not only between religion and culture (at this point sounding like Tillich) but also between God and humanity. Indeed, for Ryu, in the same way that Christ is the meeting of the divine and the human in one life in the incarnation, so there is a meeting of the divine and human creativity in great art. Art is, if you like, an incarnation of God.

So, what do we learn from this brief survey? Paul Tillich and Gordon Kaufman are more "liberal" and, in our view, "reductionist." Primarily, in their thought, religion learns from art and art can teach us religious insight, but the focus is on the human realm. And Kaufman's parallels between art and the work of theology turns theology into a creative enterprise with less emphasis on discovery. One creates rather than discovers. The assumption is that

23. Gunn, "On the Relationship," 89.

24. See Sohn, "Ryu's Pungryu Theology."

25. Sohn, "Ryu's Pungryu Theology," 182.

art is not in some sense from God and therefore revelatory of God, but instead it is a human activity where we perhaps arrive at some account of God that is pleasing. It is not heaven coming to earth, but earth arriving at some image of heaven.

We want to argue for a more robust account of art that sees the arts as a realm where God is present and showing Godself to us and, more, that we can find the reality of God behind the art. To this end, our preferences are with Maritain, Steiner, and Ryu. We see art as a place where we can truly encounter God—because art shows us the divine and therefore through art we can experience the divine.

Standing back from this discussion, our spiritual theory of art has the following shape. First, there are many forms of art, and some forms of art should be framed within a spiritual frame. We are persuaded by Wittgenstein that total generalizations about what is "true art" are not helpful. Thus, there are certain forms that are correctly described as "art" but that do not necessarily carry this spiritual dimension. However, we also take the view that some artists will create compositions that are genuinely spiritual even though the works have no explicit religious theme and even if the artists have no explicit consciousness about this dimension of their art.

Second, the act of artistic composition is analogous to the divine creativity in creation. In this respect, Steiner is right: art is akin to an *ex nihilo* (out of nothing) achievement. However, following Islamic and Thomist insights, there is also a sense in which the artist discovers the eternal and brings a sense of eternity to a particular time and place. So, perhaps rather paradoxically, creativity is both original and yet the composition can already be present in the mind of God.

Third, art points to the spiritual realm. Great art pierces the realm of eternity. Again Maritain, Steiner, and Ryu make this central. You see that a simple reductionist narrative (everything is just complex bundles of atoms that came together by accident) as utterly implausible. Great art takes you out of yourself and helps you see the eternal realm.

Having arrived at our spiritual theory of art, we conclude this chapter by reflecting on how significant this is for the Christian. Once one understands how art can work, one has a sense of the nature of the universe in which we live. It is, in short, a pointer to the spiritually infused nature of the universe.

THE SPIRITUALLY INFUSED NATURE OF THE UNIVERSE

To get to the spirituality infused nature of the universe, we need to start by pushing back on the worldview that so many people hold. The truth is that the metaphysic most people in the West believe is false. Even from a scientific perspective, it is false. This metaphysic is some version of materialism (the view that matter is all there is).

The root of this worldview is the spectacular success of science. For some advocates of this worldview, they start with a caricature of medieval Christendom. Apparently, this was a time when people believed in a three-tier universe—hell below the ground, earth in the middle, and heaven above the clouds. This was a season when epilepsy was diagnosed as demon possession. This is when spiritual explanations for the weather abounded (God is blessing us, hence the weather is good, and God is judging us, hence the weather is bad). This was the age of superstition and ignorance.

With the rise of science, we learned that the universe is explicable in terms of a mixture of calculus and classical mechanics. We arrive at a "mechanical universe." The universe is best understood as vast machine where each subsequent state is caused by the prior state. Once the clock is wound up, it will operate without any external interference. On this analogy, God is, at best, the creator who built the machine; but the idea of God interfering in the machine is not needed because the machine can just tick along all on its own.

We reach the nadir of this worldview in the work of Pierre-Simon Laplace in the eighteenth and turn of the nineteenth century. Laplace was an advocate for "causal determinism." In his *A Philosophical Essay on Probabilities*, Laplace imagined an intelligence that knew the initial configuration of atoms at the start of the universe and believed that such an intelligence would be able to see every subsequent event in the future.[26] For Laplace, everything is determined by the previous cause, and everything is reducible to atoms.

The difficulty with this worldview is simply this: originality. From Shakespeare's plays to Beethoven's Fifth Symphony, all of this, says Laplace, can be anticipated by the configuration of atoms in the universe. As Keith Ward, the Christian philosopher notes, "In general, if there are ever any new thoughts, or any sorts of things which have never happened before in the universe, then these things are in principle unpredictable by natural science (except as a sort of guess about the future, based on how things have gone in the past). Even if we could predict Laplace's brain, we could never predict his thoughts."[27]

The vast majority of contemporary physicists reject entirely the causal determinism and reductionism of Laplace. The key difference is the emergence of quantum mechanics—the study of atomic and subatomic systems. A world of neat causation disappears. Instead, we have the paradox of Heisenberg's uncertainty principle, where one cannot simultaneously speak properly of both the location and motion of an electron; this is a truth about electrons that is irreducible.[28]

Science no longer thinks of the universe as a machine. Instead, our language about nature is much more supple and open. The Cambridge physicist John Polkinghorne talks of the ten qualities of the world itself (according to the scientific view of it). They are: Elusive, Intelligible, Problematic, Surprising, Chance and Necessity, Big, Tightly Knit, Futile, Complete (within the terms it sets for itself), and Incomplete.[29] We have an openness and contingency in the universe that is a long way from a big machine.

26. Laplace, *Philosophical Essay on Probabilities.*

27. Ward, *Battle for the Soul*, 47–48.

28. Davies, *Cosmic Jackpot*, 63–64.

29. Polkinghorne, *One World.*

Perhaps the best way to think of the universe is "dappled." This is the suggestion from the philosopher of science Nancy Cartwright. She writes,

> We live our everyday lives in a dappled world quite unlike the world of fundamental particles regimented into kinds, each just like the one beside it, mindlessly marching exactly as has forever been destined. The everyday world is one where the future is open, little is certain and the unexpected intrudes into the best laid plans, where everything is different from everything else, where things change and develop, where different systems built in different ways give rise to different patterns.[30]

The best illustration of the relationship between spirit and matter is the relationship between mind and the brain. When you imagine your next vacation on a beach, this thought cannot be reduced to the neurons transmitting electro-chemical signals. The thought would not be identical to the scientific mapping of those neurons (the latter is just a mapping, while the thought is much more interesting). So, we have an analogy: there is a connection between mind and brain in the same way that there is a connection between spirit and matter. But spirit is not identical to matter. It is a reality that transcends and works through the material.

With most events in the world, two forms of causation are operating simultaneously and intertwined. There is physical causation, which science describes helpfully, and there is spiritual causation, which includes everything from thoughts (which cannot be reduced to simply brain activity) to angels. The physical causes are visible and measured by science. The spiritual causes are less visible and often subject to careful interpretation from within a religious tradition, but they are compatible with modern science.

Once it is seen that there is a spiritual dimension to life that is as real as the material dimension to life, then we can see the importance of learning about this spiritual realm. The Christian claim is that Jesus—the Eternal Word—is not simply the source of the world but also an authority on the spiritual realm. Jesus

30. Cartwright and Ward, "Dethronement of Laws in Science," 26.

reveals to humanity the nature of the spiritual realm and how it interacts with the material. The Gospel of Mark starts with people marveling at the authority that Jesus exercised as a teacher in the synagogue (see Mark 1:21–28). Jesus knows about the realm of the angelic and demonic forces. Christians want to claim that to be fully human one should learn about the reality of this spiritual realm. Christians also want to claim that Jesus is our guide to this spiritual realm. Living completely aware of the multi-layered nature of the world is to live fully into life.

Art is an important way into the spiritually infused nature of reality. For anyone seeking to witness to faith in a secular world, art is a precious and valuable tool. Art can be seen in many ways, but in this chapter, we have argued for a spiritual theory of art. This is the recognition that art can sometimes be a vehicle that helps us to engage with the transcendent, which is beyond the material.

The capacity to appreciate art is a skill that needs to be learned. This is true of all skills. To appreciate a great meal, one needs a guide who can explain everything that went into the dish; to appreciate the game of baseball, you need a guide who can explain what the home base is; to appreciate a piece of classical music, you need a guide who can gently help you hear the nuance in the piece; and so it is with art. Although the untrained eye can still see something, the gift of training is that you see the form, the detail, the paintbrush strokes, and the careful use of color. Spending time in art galleries is part of the training. Reading a guide book can help. And then just sitting with a piece, allowing your eye to travel around every inch of the piece from different vantage points, can bring you to a place where you have truly experienced the piece of art.

In the next chapter, Anne Bent will introduce to you the extraordinary world of old master drawings. She is our guide into the world of appreciation of this form of art. Then, once this is completed, we can start to allow the art to be a vehicle for disclosure of the divine. One can sense just a little about the miracle of living and life through the art and the meditations later in this book.

CHAPTER THREE

Understanding an Old Master Drawing

"The intuitive mind is a sacred gift and the rational mind is a faithful servant. We have created a society that honors the servant and has forgotten the gift."[1]

ON PERCEIVING AN OLD MASTER DRAWING

There are numerous lenses through which to view art. Our goal here is to encourage the reader to access their soul through their eyes as they experience taking in the image in an old master drawing. Like prayer, this kind of seeing takes practice. Before we delve into this way of reading a drawing, the basics of what an old master drawing is and how it is composed will be covered.

The role of drawing within the production of a final work of art took on a significance all its own by the first part of the sixteenth century in Italy. The importance or primacy of drawing as an art form valid unto itself varied from region to region, from period to period in Italy and other parts of Europe. Drawings were made for different purposes. Nonetheless, drawings were valued and collected as works of art themselves from that time forward.

1. This quote is sometimes attributed to Einstein. Whether or not he said it, the words contain much insight.

To read and fully experience an old master drawing it is useful to understand the techniques, media, types of paper, and stages of *disegno* (design) used in the execution of the work. In this volume the reader will primarily encounter Italian old master drawings with a few drawings from other parts of Europe.

Throughout time, young artists have been apprenticed to established masters. As implements and media became more varied, the novices were taught to use them, practicing basic techniques until they became accomplished at each one. Master artists attracted young students who worked for food, a safe place to sleep, and the chance to learn. Sometimes large workshops developed if the master was well recognized and had sufficient commissions to support it. The papacy was often the primary source of work, as seen in the exceptional Sistine chapel, but commissions also came from members of the aristocracy.

THE ROLE OF DRAWING

> In general drawing remained in Italy an extremely important element in the training of an artist, both from a technical and an intellectual point of view: the best way available to afford the complexity of figurative expression, and to proceed smoothly on the difficult (and often long and winding) path which leads from invention to execution, from the very first idea to the finished work of art. . . . Drawing becomes the fundamental tool in an artist's hands to exercise the widest and most effective control of every aspect of his professional activity.[2]

Drawings made in Europe in the sixteenth through the beginning of the nineteenth centuries were used as tools. They were primary to the working method of the artist. The purpose of the drawings was to assist the artist in visualizing details of the composition, whether it would be a fresco, panel, a painting, or sculpture in its final form.

2. Tofani, "Role of Drawing."

This introduction will cover the types of drawings, the media, and in the case of Italian drawings in particular, the stages of drawing that could be employed to achieve full preparation prior to beginning the final work of art.

The way each artist uses drawing and the style of that drawing depended on his or her unique working technique. Paper was handmade in individual sheets. It was expensive, so often both sides of the sheet were used. The two sides could be unrelated in subject or for different aspects of the same final work. The front side is termed the "recto" while the back side is called the "verso." In the papermaking process a pulp was made of water, linen, cloth fabrics, and sometimes wood pulp or other plant fibers. It was beaten to a smooth consistency. This pulp was then heated so the mixture could be placed evenly on a rectangular screen. The mixture was lightly pressed causing the water to drain through the screen. While the mixture was still damp, a design was sometimes imprinted into the mixture using a tool a bit like a cold branding iron. As the pulp dried it retained the design, known as a watermark. These watermarks were unique to each locale and period of time, so they were distinct. The watermark is usually only visible by holding the paper up to the light; it is rarely discernible within the drawn surface of the paper. Since the design of the watermark was only used for a limited time in a particular region, it can be used to help determine the approximate date and place where a sheet was made. This is important for scholarship as it can indicate which artists could have made the drawing based on the place and timeframe in which the paper was made and the known history of particular artists.

The attribution of "old master drawings" is complex, as it can sometimes be difficult to determine which artist or school of artists created a drawing. Those works were rarely signed by the draughtsman since they were just tools used in the creative process. Drawings scholars rely on watermarks, the type of paper under consideration, and the subject of the drawing, which may correlate to other known work by an artist. Since paper was made by hand, it is possible sometimes to identify it as coming from a particular region based on the materials used in making it, even if there is no visible watermark to identify it.

Art historians may also elicit fellow scholars' opinions to make an attribution. Further, like other fields of scholarship, the knowledge base expands over time. Scholars can disagree over an attribution. Attributions also evolve as new experts rise in recognition within the field.

Another way that drawings can be attributed is by using the small marks that appear on the edge or even the reverse of a drawing. These little marks are called collectors' stamps. In earlier eras collectors had a small, uniquely-designed stamp made which, when inked and applied to a drawing, indicated their ownership of that drawing. These marks have been extensively studied and cataloged. Drawings connoisseurs pride themselves on being able to identify the collectors' stamps in their area of expertise.

The provenance of a given drawing is the history of who owned it. This may indicate for what period of time it was in a particular collection. Collectors' stamps often provide this chain of possession. Research on any drawing that has ever been in a public sale or been included in a published article can also tell us more about that work. The Courtauld library in London is devoted to retaining all such published information in vast archives, both actual and virtual.

THE MEDIA OF DRAWINGS

Turning to the media of drawings, artists used different materials, including ink, usually brown, although black or grey ink could also be made. Chalks were black, white, or red. Gouache is an opaque white liquid used as an accent which when employed in a composition is referred to as white heightening. Washes could be made by diluting ink or crushing chalk into water. The wash creates the effect of volume, atmosphere, and solid mass. For example, in the Madonna del Popolo red chalk was used to create a tinted wash, as seen in upper section of that drawing. Artists drew with quills, sharpened metal nibs, brushes, and chalks.

In some of the drawings pictured, the viewer will notice places where one of the figures has its head, hand, arm, or shoulders in several different drawn positions. When we see multiple positions of a body part in a drawing, it is referred to as pentimenti. This intentional placement of the same hand, for example, in several positions close together helps the draughtsman visualize which placement will look the best for his or her purpose in the final version. Pentimenti are found in Mary's hands in the *Madonna del Popolo* (p. 77). It is also found in the lower center foreground of that drawing. There, a monk is kissing the ground in response to appearance of the holy group above. The viewer will notice that the monk's head and shoulders are drawn in several different positions just above one another.

Another feature used in these working drawings is when a grid is drawn over the whole composition. This "squaring for transfer" technique made it possible for the artist or the workshop to enlarge the drawn image on to a wall by proportionately enlarging the work within each square in equal measure to create the composition in a larger format. This addition of a grid is visible in the *Dormition of the Virgin* by G. M. Morandi and in *Saint Ambrose Baptizing Saint Augustine* by Cirro Ferri.

Old master drawings were made for various purposes, depending on what the artist needed at the time. There is a progression of complexity, which is as follows. A drawing that was a sketch using just one medium, like that of *Charity* by Raphael, was likely an early sketch to formulate the elements and layout of the subject. A later-stage drawing might use several media, such as black chalk under drawing with brown ink and ink wash to create a more substantial image. The next stage might be a drawing that filled the whole sheet, whether in one or several media. A late-stage drawing would be a fully developed image that might also be squared for transfer, indicating that the composition was going to be enlarged for the final work. Artists also created beautiful, finished drawings as a record (*ricordo*) of the work for themselves or sometimes for their patrons. These *ricordi* may have been a gift or simply part of the agreed-upon work. Draughtsmen sadly were often paid meager wages, only little by little as the work progressed.

ENCOUNTERING THE IMAGES

This summary of the basic elements of "old master drawings" will assist the reader, informing her how and why drawings were made as they appear in this volume. The focus here, as stated in prior chapters, is to encounter the drawn image as a source of personal reflection and devotion. The impact and presumed meaning of a drawing will differ from one individual viewer to the next. Each individual's eye has an aesthetic of viewing that is unique to them. One person might respond primarily to the wash technique; another might respond most readily to the figures' facial expressions, deriving meaning by what they convey.

There is an overarching theology of viewing art, which I propose starts with spending time immersing oneself in a work, in this case in an old master drawing, wherein resides the potential for an encounter with the divine. The drawings in this volume were specifically chosen because this access to the divine reality is readily available within the images, be it the *Annunciation* or the *Deposition*. The reader who can see beyond the rendering of the image into its deeper meaning about the human condition, one that we have created through our own actions in history, can also access Gods presence in the tender revelation of the *Annunciation* and the depth of loss in the *Deposition*. God is in all of this, we understand, through his compassion and ultimate sacrifice for us. These images give us a window or doorway into that aspect of the reality of our existence.

It is hoped that the basic information above will free the reader to engage more fully with each image over time, experiencing the divine within the work at hand. Again, these old master drawings contain recognizable images or scenes created with paper, ink, and a quill. The image then invokes reactions, thoughts, and feelings in the viewer. This creation is a remarkable achievement. Through this act of creation, the artist discovers or taps into the eternal, rendering it in a form that can give the viewer a transcendent vision. So, in this way the visual experience can become a silent dialog with the viewer and, by extension, with God. The viewer may experience engaging with the image in this way as unlimited, without the constraints of time of language.

A POSTSCRIPT: EXPLAINING A PASSION

I have explained how old master drawings were made and some of their uses. In conclusion, I wish to share with the reader how this passion developed in my life. I first encountered them through my lifelong friend Suzanne Folds McCullagh, whose entire career was spent in the department of prints and drawings at the Art Institute of Chicago. Once I had learned how to safely handle the drawings, I was allowed to peruse boxes of drawings from the vault in that study room. That was a wonderful learning experience. Also, I became a member of the support committee to that department, so I was exposed to all the works presented at each committee meeting. Those works could come from any of the last six centuries of graphic art. It was a great exposure to the breadth of graphic art.

The art that appeals to any viewer can do so based on different qualities and reasons. What was primary for me was to be moved by a drawing. So, the subject and especially the rendering or technique used had to have an impact on me. Being a Christian, I was particularly captured by drawings of religious subjects if they were well drawn and evocative. My preference is for drawings that are beautiful or striking and have an emotional impact. Secondary considerations included the condition of the work and its authenticity, both of which can be verified by experts.

In any collection of drawings, the collector's unique aesthetic gives a particular flavor to his or her collection. While the focus here is on drawings of Christian subjects, I have also collected other kinds of drawings, landscapes and figure drawings that are of secular subjects. Again, my primary motivation has been to find drawings that evoke an emotional response to the image. Drawings differ from other forms of fine art because they are generally small enough to be held by an individual and shared with another person. This is often an intimate experience as the two viewers are drawn into the image. Sharing one's reactions and thoughts is a wonderful part of that experience.

In some ways I'm fortunate not to have had any academic training in old master drawings because my reactions are not complicated by trying to judge all of the aspects of a drawing, such as those explained earlier in this chapter. I have the freedom to simply take in the drawing and react to it. Certainly, questions come up and need to be entertained as part of the overall process. When viewing others' drawings, it is a delight to ask questions and engage in conversation about them.

When I began to purchase drawings in the 1970s it was for the museum. Then I gave prints as gifts to my family and was delighted by their responses. Finally, in the 1980s, I started buying drawings for myself. Once at a formal dinner party I was seated next to Phillipe de Rothschild who asked me why I preferred Italian old master drawings to others. Taken aback I answered that it is because they are so beautiful. So, in the end these drawings provide a sense of beauty, of human accomplishment and ingenuity, of the best and worst of human behavior, and a way to access the Divine, who underscores all of this. For me, there is no more compelling reason to spend my time and resources than this experience.

Meditations

Adam and Eve Mourning the Dead Able by J. C. Loth

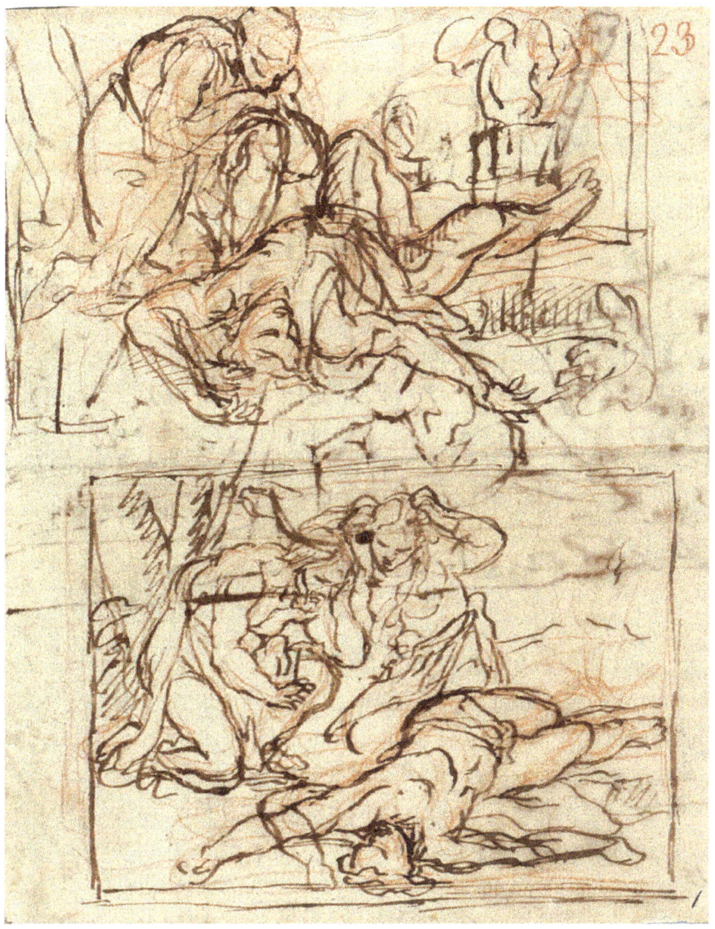

This reflection is based on the lower of the two red chalk drawings by Loth. I cannot imagine the sorrow of coming upon my son beaten to death! "How could this have happened?" These must be some of the thoughts running through the tormented minds of Adam and Eve. We know that denial and disbelief are common first reactions to the news of an unexpected death. We all forget our own mortality, perhaps because we need to suspend the knowledge of our own death in order to carry out our daily life and work. We can see the torment Adam and Eve are feeling as they kneel by Abel. Eve has interlaced her fingers in her hair. She may be readying to tear her hair out in her grief and disbelief.

In the context of faith, presented with such a brutal murder, we may well wonder, how could a loving God allow this to happen to my beloved son? Can I now find any comfort from a God who cannot prevent such a thing from happening? Or, does this mean that my faith is in vain and futile? One might conclude that such a tragedy as that one, pictured above in red chalk, indicates that there is no God. Or worse than that, Adam and Eve may wonder, "Has something we've done caused God to abandon us?"

Where does one turn in a time of such immense confusion and pain? Only the Holy Spirit can shine through that pain to aid us at such a moment. Perhaps you have experienced this in your own life. It is possible to recover from such a loss through the love and ministrations of a faithful community.

PRAYER

Dear God, we know that brutality and violence are part of the sinful actions of humans. When such behavior causes death, especially of someone we hold dear, we are confused, frightened, angry, and left feeling loss beyond words. Help us to remember that your love is bigger than these human actions. Bring us from a place of utter despair to the realization that you will help us accept and survive such an experience. We pray, Lord, bring the Holy Spirit to us to comfort us as we mourn such an unspeakable loss. Amen.

Adoration of the Shepherds by G. M. Bedoli

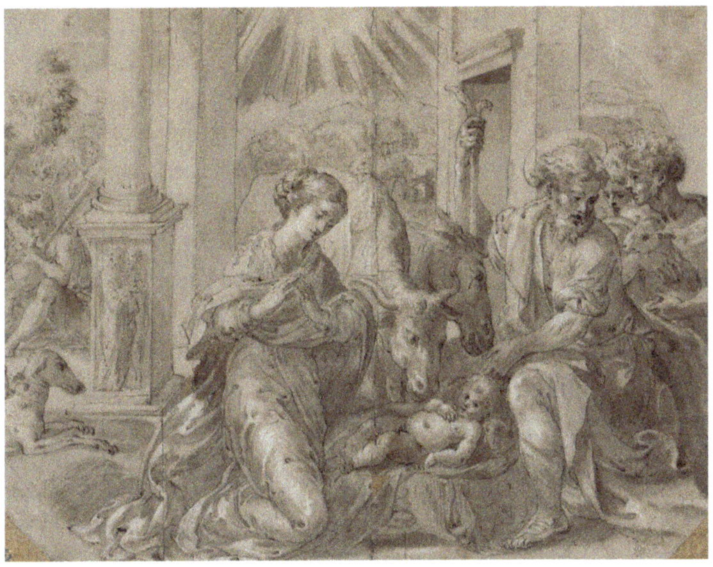

In this intimate rendering of the Nativity, the ox and the donkey seem to be stirred by the sight of the baby Jesus every bit as much as the people around him. The cow almost appears to be smiling down at the little child. Mary and Joseph kneel in reverence on either side of their son, their cloaks flowing dramatically around them. A shepherd at the far left of the drawing plays his bagpipe, though no one seems to be listening. The setting here derives from the Golden Legend, a popular mediaeval commentary on the location of the Nativity, which described it as taking place in the ruins of the Roman temple to Apollo.[1] According to the Golden Legend, the building was prophesied to fall to ruins the moment a virgin conceived a child. Clearly a miracle has occurred, as the old temple now houses the Holy Family.

1. This information is courtesy of Thomas Williams, an art historian and author, who has helped edit these entries. So widely known was the Golden Legend interpretation that visual allusions to it can be found in depictions of the Nativity as late as the eighteenth century.

Another important aspect of the Temple of Apollo is that it signifies that Apollo will be the future of Rome. In our drawing the birth of the baby Jesus and his life will provide a different and certain future for his followers. The rays of divine light from the top edge of the drawing presage Jesus being the light of the world. This light reminds us of God's light in giving Jesus to the world. The cow smiling as it drops his head near the babe is not the common response of a barn animal to a strange sight. Perhaps the cow's reaction is an indication that nature itself will respond very positively to Jesus' presence in the world. The shepherds depicted to the viewers right have brought their lambs foretelling that Jesus is the lamb of God. The shepherds are looking with wonder at the scene before them. Jesus entering the world will cause many who see him to wonder at his actions and words. So here we see several indications in this remarkable drawing that Jesus will be a very important presence and influence on the world that he is born into—and, by extension, on our world.

What does it mean to you that our Lord and Savior was born in a humble shelter meant only for livestock? One cannot miss the contrast between the Holy One's arrival and the poor conditions of his birthplace, a last resort for his family, yet safe from the dangers of the night outside. What is it that gives us a sense of ultimate protection from the threats of the outside world? Do we have such a place? What can and should we do about those people in our area who have no shelter yet desperately need it? As Christians, we are compelled to remember those who live out on the streets, while we are likely safe and secure indoors. The birth of Jesus in a place not fit for human habitation is a powerful example of how we must accept and make do with those circumstances in life that we cannot change. Mary and Joseph gratefully accept what small comforts they are offered as they must contend with the biggest event in human lives, the birth of a child. How is their acceptance of the only simple shelter available in their time of need a lesson for us in our twenty-first-century world?

PRAYER

Holy Jesus, we need to learn from your birth in lowly conditions how to accept our own circumstances of comfort and ease or of deprivation in the place where we started our lives and where we live now. Please help us transcend the limiting elements of that place to become more fully the people you want us to be, ready to act in the world according to your will. Amen.

Avenging Angel by Cecco Bravo

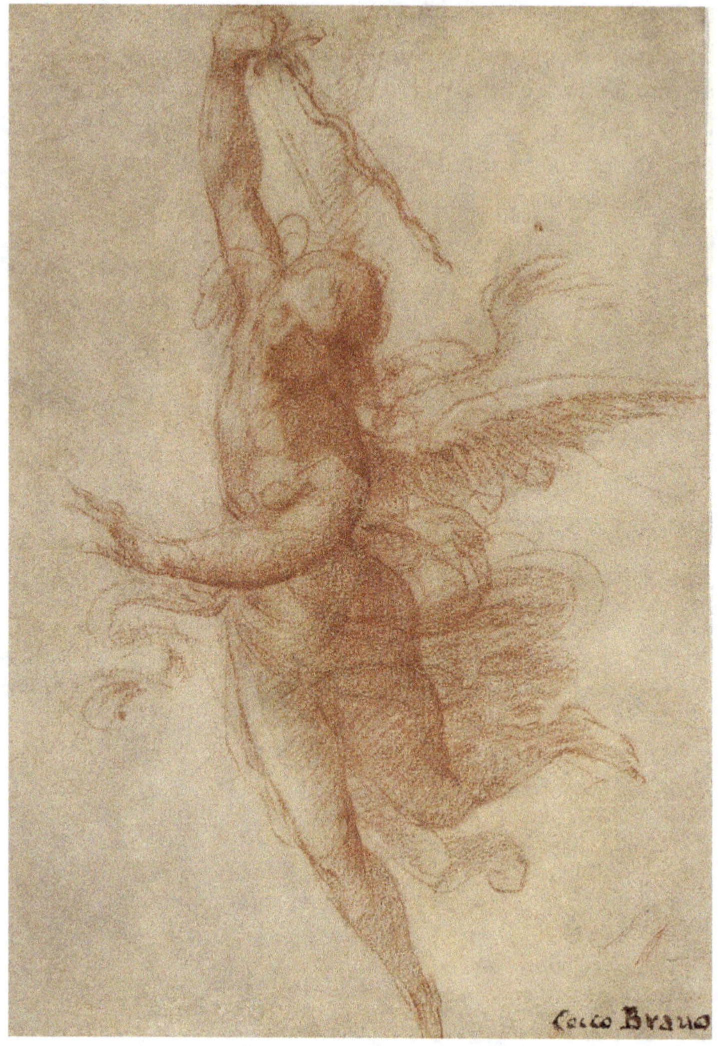

This red chalk figure of a fearsome avenging angel looks as though he could twist right off the page, were he to strike down with the serpentine sword in his hand. The angel is wildly in motion, defying the two-dimensional constraints of the paper (it seems to me that he could snap out into space spinning as he went). It is both exciting and frightening to imagine this angel's movement and intentions. Is he poised to strike in anger or vengeance? The angel has the power to act as God's agent for God's purposes. *We* cannot exact vengeance without being unlawful. We need to leave ultimate vengeance in God's hands. There is a temptation to strike out in anger, but we need to consider whether this has ever produced a positive outcome. Regret is the likely outcome when we cannot curb our unbridled anger. When has this ever produced a positive outcome? It is more probable that we regret the action of unbridled emotion if we do not curb it.

The charge of anger can urgently demand expression but usually only exacerbates the problem. Instead, we ask that God's hand should stay the possibility of real harm. Then, a more measured path to address and heal the rift can be put into place when we have suspended the worst of the potential damage that we wish we could execute. If we are able to contain our strong emotions, then we may transform, own, or let go of our anger. Or, as the Buddhists teach, we can even befriend our anger in order to learn from it or let it teach us in quiet contemplation. In order to do so, we must not act out but rather sit with the intense feelings.

Let this dynamic image be a warning about the dangers of unleashed anger in us. If we have ever craved revenge, we also know the power of that emotion. While some may experience getting revenge as sweet, especially if it appears to have brought no consequences, it will cause us harm when our actions are examined at the end of our lives. Let us remember that God said, "Vengeance is Mine" (Deuteronomy 32:35). Then we can rely on his judgment of us and of the offender.

PRAYER

Lord, help us to stay our anger and our desire for vengeance, no matter how justified these may seem in the heat of the moment. We rely on your judgment to show us another way to approach the situation that can produce a more positive outcome for all concerned. We give thanks for your guidance in this moment and always. In Jesus' name we pray. Amen.

Cain and Able by Lodovico Cardi (called Cigoli)

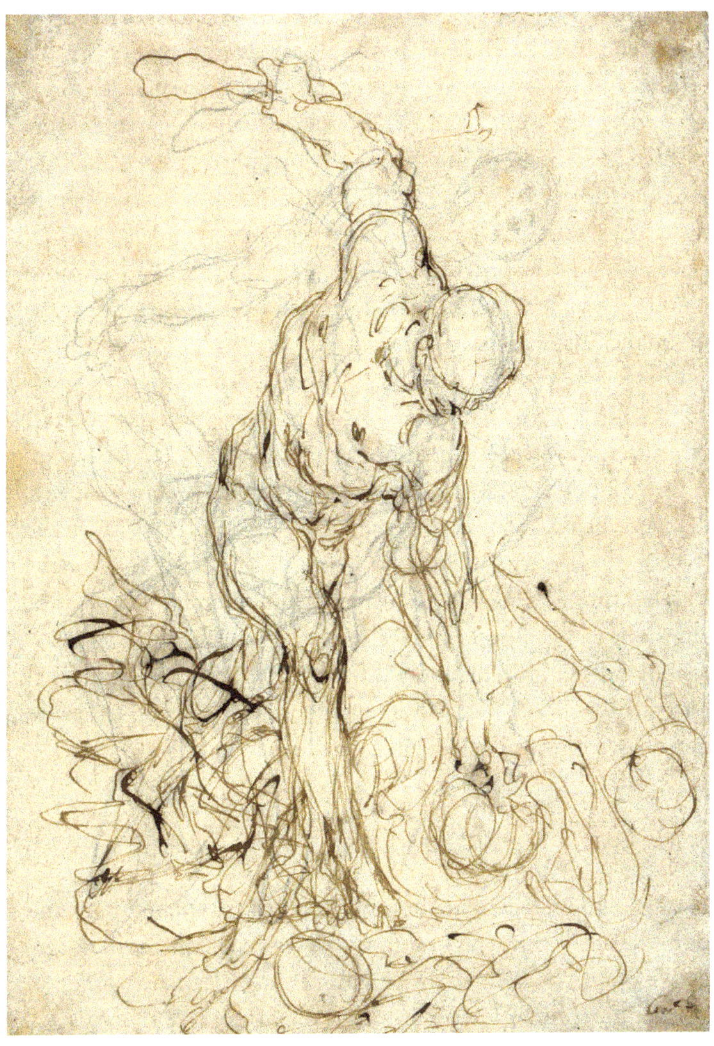

In this finely drawn image we see a man, club in hand, beating another man on the ground. That lower part of the image is a series of circular shapes and wavy lines, indicating extreme motion in this lower figure. We know that Cain is in the process of beating his brother Able to death out of jealous, uncontrollable rage. That this murder could occur in the first family is our cue to look very seriously at our own anger, how and when it can become uncontrollable rage. We are all capable of it, and may God help those who have been the victims of this rage throughout time. We understand that those who have experienced violence, especially as children, are more likely to be violent themselves. In these times we are surrounded by the spread of violence so that we are forced to confront our own part in the proliferation of it. Is it possible for us, as Christians, to turn the tide of harm? Can we show others how our faith allows us different ways to respond to seemingly ubiquitous violence? Would that we could simply turn our swords into plowshares, as in Isaiah 2:4.

Perhaps we must start with prayer, when we rely on God to cool our anger, we can then ask the Holy Spirit for the grace to seek other ways to interact if possible or to walk away until we can gain control of our emotions again. God has told us that human wrath does not bring about divine righteousness. It is not our place to punish the wicked. Only the righteous judge can do that in a way that is fitting: "Vengeance is mine" (Deuteronomy 32:35). When anger flares up around us, it's tempting to run from it or even join in, but we are called to witness to peace. We can pray for the judgment to know when to intervene and when we must protect ourselves and those with us in a given situation.

PRAYER

Lord, we know that anger and rage are part of the human condition. We need your help to control ourselves. Please Lord, also give us the words to calm angry situations that arise in our daily life. You are the source of peace and lover of harmony amongst us, your creatures. Bring us to a deeper knowledge of that peace so we can use it to assist others, loving one another as ourselves, to the glory of your Name. Amen.

Charity by Raphael

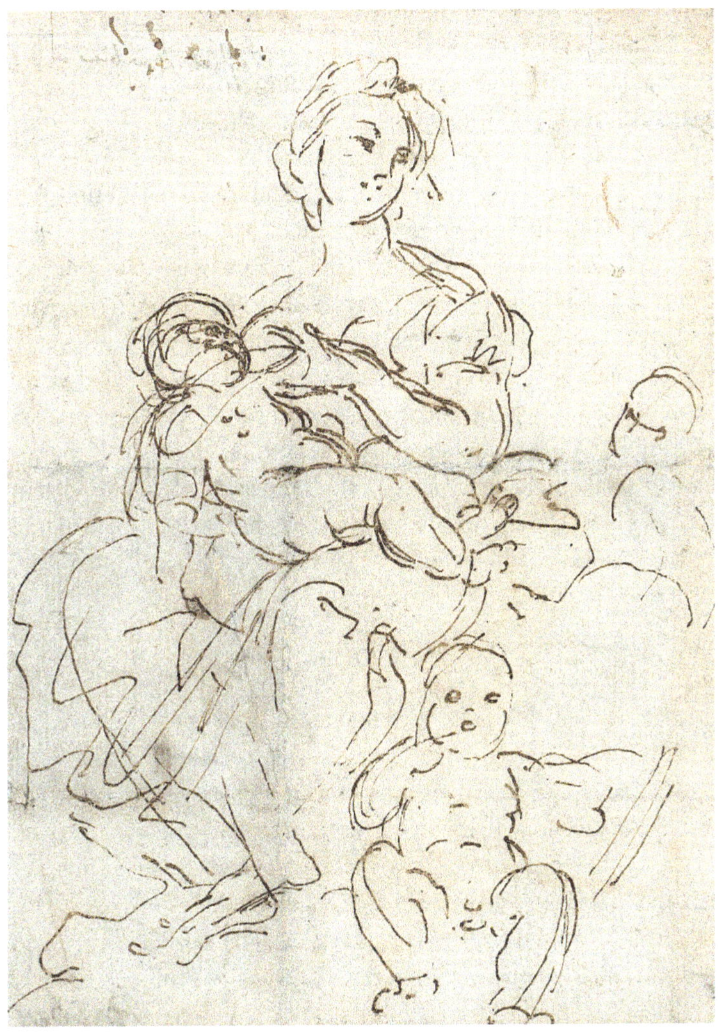

A woman representing Charity holds her breast to a large infant, who suckles while resting in her lap. Two other small ones look out, presumably waiting their turns to be fed. We do not know whether all of these are her own children; the title of the drawing suggests that this woman is feeding all the little ones who are pictured there, which would definitely qualify as abundant love, in my estimation. While wet nurses were common in Raphael's time, art historians presume that the proper title of the drawing is *Charity*.

Charity is a Christian attribute, one that we strive to employ in our daily living. Charity derives from the Latin word *caritas*, meaning love for all. As Jesus taught us, "What you did for the least of these, you did for me." Also, he commands us to love our neighbors as ourselves. Like many others, I could spend my lifetime just trying to fulfill this one commandment.

What is it in your experience that inspires charity in your actions? Do you have favorite charities that you support? Are you willing to receive charity when you are in need? It isn't always easy for us to accept charity. I know that the devil is at work when there is an opportunity to be charitable, and I wish to withhold that act of kindness instead. When are we able to do the right thing for charity's sake, and what specifically tempts us to withhold that charity? How can we turn to Jesus and ask him to help us turn that self-centeredness into genuine charity? Prayer helps.

PRAYER

Dear Lord, you ask us to love one another as you have loved us and to love our neighbor as ourselves. You know that these are truly challenging commandments for us who are weak and selfish people. So, we pray that you will assist us to be generous, fair, and loving with all those around us, especially when we are feeling selfish, just not interested or even repelled by those in need of charity. We trust in your loving patience with us and hope that you will guide us in all of our ways, today and always. Amen.

Christ Bearing the Cross, Appearing to a Man, Attended by an Angel by Il Cavaliere D'Arpino

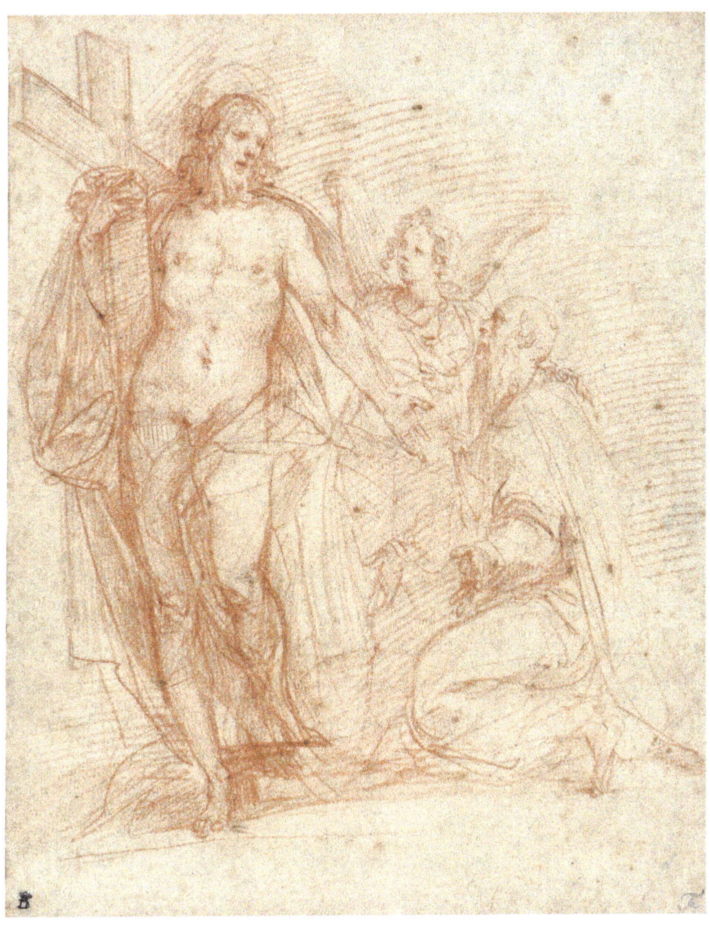

"If you would call on the Savior, the Lord Jesus Christ, you shall be saved" (Acts 16:13)

In the red chalk drawing of the resurrected Jesus, we see him addressing—perhaps also blessing—a kneeling, bearded man. An attending angel looks on. Imagine how you might respond to see our risen Lord walking by victoriously, carrying his cross, fully alive and as kind and healing a presence as ever existed! Wouldn't you feel lifted up from all burdens you were carrying the moment before? Through our faith, and because of his resurrection, we have been made a people renewed and redeemed! What an immeasurable gift he has given us.

During the COVID-19 epidemic, in answer to the question, "How are you?" I was blessed to reply, "I am vertical and grateful." Grateful because Jesus has risen from the dead, building a real bridge between us and our Creator. What multiple blessings he has bestowed on us, through his life's teachings, in his humble death on the cross, his descent to the depths of hell, and his resurrection. All of this so that we may be released from the eternal hold of death. Hallelujah! We are liberated because Jesus is the living God, who will dwell in all of those who earnestly seek his presence in their lives. We can offer ourselves in his service in joyful acceptance of all he has done for us.

PRAYER

Dear Lord, assist us to become more like the kneeling man in the image, who opens his arms at the wonderment of your presence. Help us to look up to you as the author of our salvation. Give us the grace to accept all that your love means in our lives. We can only do this through your help. Empower us to be more like you as we experience the ordinary daily events in our lives. Amen.

Christ on the Cross by Il Cavaliere D'Arpino

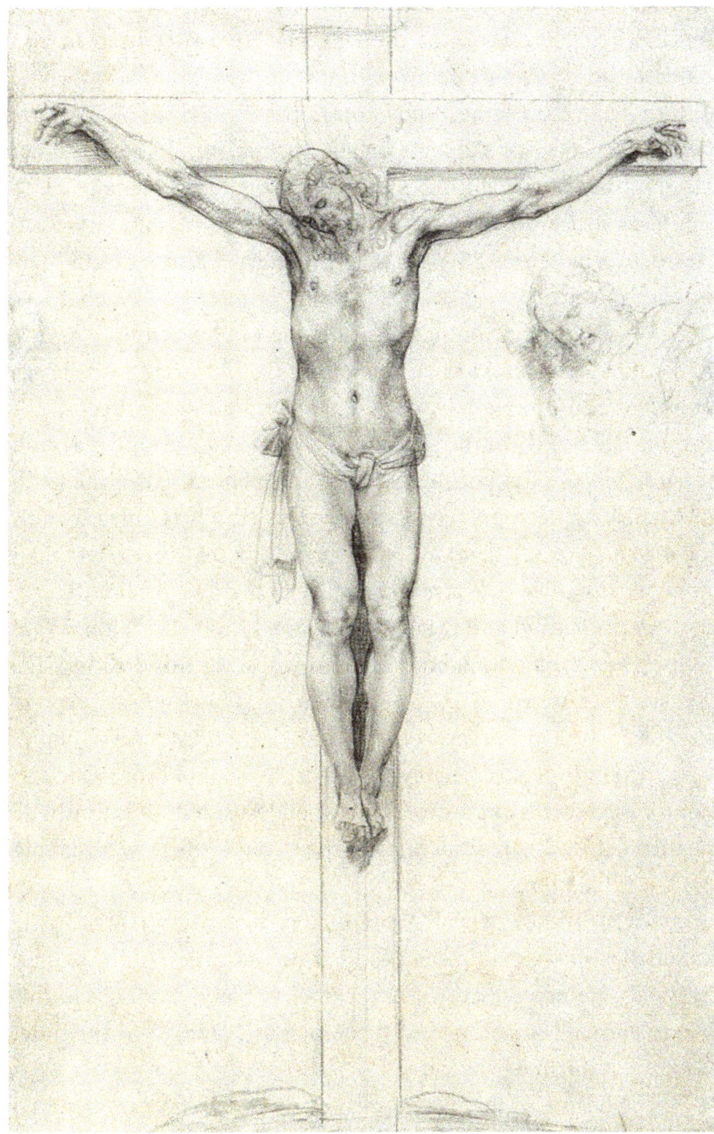

This beautifully rendered drawing of the crucifixion was done in delicately handled black chalk. Christ's body is limp, emphasizing that he has already died. There is a certain final stillness to the body, deftly indicated by the position of the head, arms, and feet. The beautiful shading in black chalk shows Jesus' lean, superbly formed figure. Further, the drawing places Christ's head in two different positions just below the joint of the cross. Then there is a third sketch of the head position to the viewer's right. This use of multiple layers of elements is called *pentimenti*. It indicates that D'Arpino is experimenting with exactly where he wants to place the head in the final work. This drawing was preparatory for a fresco, executed in 1588/89 in the Monastery, Certosa di San Martino in Naples.

We see here the body of a young man in his prime. In trying to comprehend the act of crucifixion of that innocent man, Jesus, one may find one's eye wandering over the drawing, deeply absorbing the beauty of the shading and of the figure. One may find it hard, because the image is so deftly created, to accept the truth of what this image portrays. Namely, this man was killed for following the journey that God, his Father, had set him on less than three years earlier. The riveting quality of the image belies the act of powerful hatred and fear that motivated this crucifixion. What feelings and thoughts come to mind as you study this drawing? Do you see Jesus as gentle? To my eye, there is no hint in Jesus' expression or posture of the agony that such a death must have wrought. Crucified individuals actually died of asphyxiation. I speculate and hope, based on his expression, that when Jesus said, "It is finished," he then felt God's presence and comfort even while he was making his last exhalation.

I wish I knew why D'Arpino chose to portray Christ being so much at peace. Notice that there is no indication of the wound in Jesus' side nor the crown of thorns. No blood is shown in this image either. The absence of those details may add to the quiet serenity of the image.

The beauty of this drawing compels us to reflect on the final act in Christ's life. The portrayal in this drawing is unique because it is so pure, serene, and bloodless. Think on what this sacrifice means in your own faith. Is it something you remember regularly or more often during Eastertide? Not all Christians have images of the crucifixion with Jesus' body on the cross in their homes and churches. We might well ask, why is that? Are we missing something by focusing on the cross devoid of the body of our Lord? This piques my curiosity. What thoughts do you have?

PRAYER

Dear Lord Jesus, we remember the sacrifice that you made by hanging on the cross, although you were innocent of any crime. We may prefer not to look at your lifeless body on that cross because it causes us pain. We are not like those saints who experience ecstasy when they contemplate and hold a crucifix in hand. We need you to help us remember the sacrifice you made for us, for our sinful lives, that day you died on Golgotha. Bring us through prayer your grace to accept humbly the gift you freely bestowed on us. Further, lift us into the frame of mind where we can be of service to others through your gift to us. In your name we ask this. Amen.

Christ Washing the Feet of the Apostles **by G. Muziano**

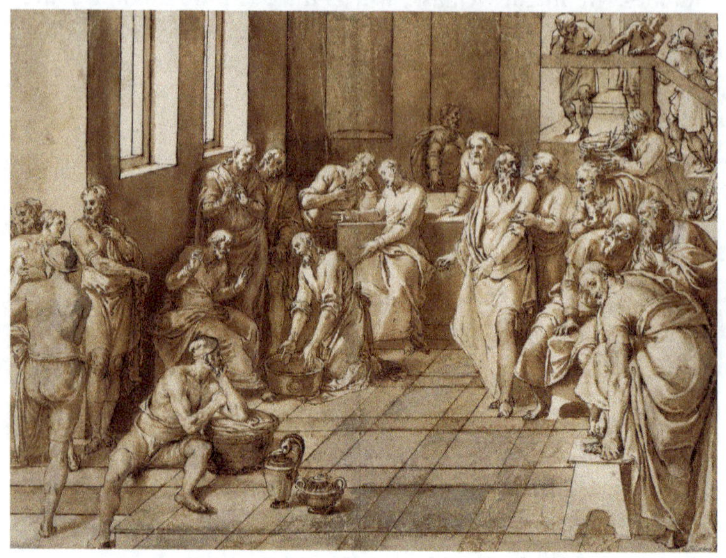

A large group is gathered in a domestic interior in this brown ink and ink wash work. The occasion is of the utmost significance, for it is the beginning of the Last Supper of our Lord. It may take the viewer a moment to find Jesus, who is kneeling in the left center of the picture, imploring Peter to allow him to wash his feet. Jesus wears a towel around his waist, as described in John's Gospel (John 13:1–38). All around him, the disciples are gesturing and discussing his actions. The washing of feet at mealtime was an ancient Jewish custom, but the job was considered menial and usually given to the lowest ranking servant, not to the host, and certainly not to the disciples' rabbi and teacher. That is why Peter objects so strongly to Jesus preforming this task. As we know, Jesus finally gives Peter an ultimatum, "Unless I wash your feet, you cannot share life with me." Then Peter exuberantly asks to have not only his feet but also his head and hands washed, but Jesus replies that the rest of Peter's body is already clean.

Have you ever experienced someone washing your feet, perhaps at a Maundy Thursday service in Holy Week? As a culture we tend to wear sandals only in the summertime, so our lower limbs are not covered by the dust and dirt of the road as they were in biblical times. Today, the baring of one's feet is an exposure that can be uncomfortable for some, perhaps even embarrassing. Nevertheless, we understand the importance of this ritual gesture, so we manage our own reactions. It is humbling to have a priest touch, wash, and dry your feet. Once at a service, I saw a parishioner kneel down to wash the priest's feet after he had washed hers. I was impressed by that role-reversal. Can we be both the servant and the honored guest? Are there situations that require this dual role in our Christian lives? Consider which activities are humbling for you and which put you in a lead role? Which of these positions is more natural for you? Which role is more challenging? Finally, how can we rely on Jesus' teachings to guide us as we accept these dual roles and utilize them in our daily lives? How often might we be required to be either the leader or the servant in a situation? Is it possible to be both within the same interaction? Are serving and leading part of being a deeply committed Christian everyday life?

PRAYER

Dear Jesus, sometimes you ask things of us that radically challenge our way of thinking. Help us to accept these requests, relying on your love to uphold us as we stretch into the new actions that you want from us. Transform our fear or complete reluctance into true faith in your support and guidance, that you will give us the strength, resources, and determination to follow your lead. This we ask in your name. Amen.

Dormition of the Virgin **by G. M. Morandi**

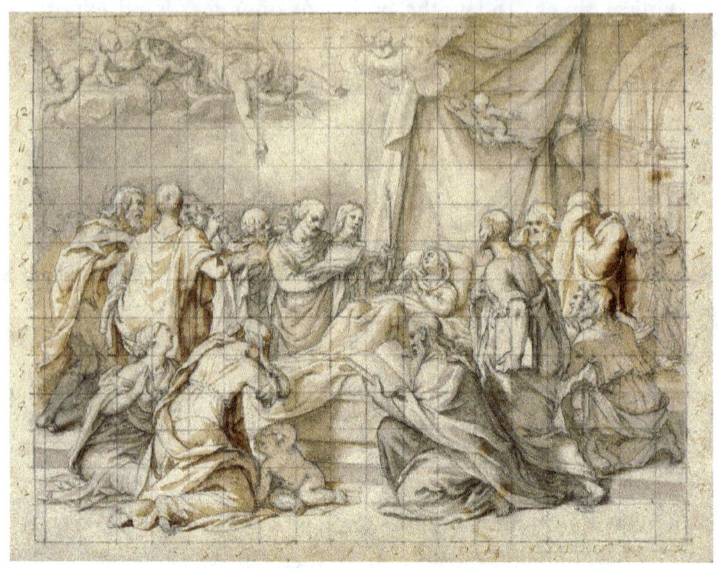

The Dormition of the Virgin in the Catholic and Orthodox traditions is the unique moment when Mary is bodily assumed up into heaven without dying first. It is a representation of how pure Mary was that she could ascend without death or decay.

Look at the drawing. The disciples, including some of the women followers, are present with Mary. They each show their own reactions to her end time. She alone sees Jesus and some angels as her son reaches down to bring her into the heavenly realm. This tradition singles Mary out as the only human who had the experience of not dying before she is risen. The rest of humanity does not have this privileged experience. We must die before we can rise.

Being present with a dying person is a holy experience. Death comes in a myriad of ways, sometimes gently, sometimes in loud anguish, and sometimes with a godly light that illumines the face of the departing one. On occasion, people see Jesus or other loved ones coming for them, or they see a beauty that is beyond our ability to perceive as they pass beyond our worldly existence. There are also experiences of fighting death or intense expressions of fear and dread. Often, unless families intervene, the end-of-life experience is now muted through the use of medications. Those are individual choices, though can sometimes be an absolute necessity.

What we witness when we attend a death has a lasting impact on us. In what ways does God assist us in carrying on after the death of a loved one? Sadly, our culture does not honor or support the bereaved. We do not wear black or even a black armband to signify that we are in mourning. Thus, we have lost the customs that helped provide a respectful approach by others, imbued with kindness for those who have suffered a loss.

PRAYER

Dear Lord, even though we know what you have done for each of us in your crucifixion, coming back from the dead to win our freedom from a permanent grave; still, it is so hard for us to let a loved one go! Help us to accept their departure to be with you and our Father. Help all of us to be kind, sympathetic, and of service to those among us who mourn, as they come to an acceptance of their loss through the comfort of the Holy Spirit. In Jesus' name we pray. Amen.

First Family before a Shelter
by Baccio Bandinelli

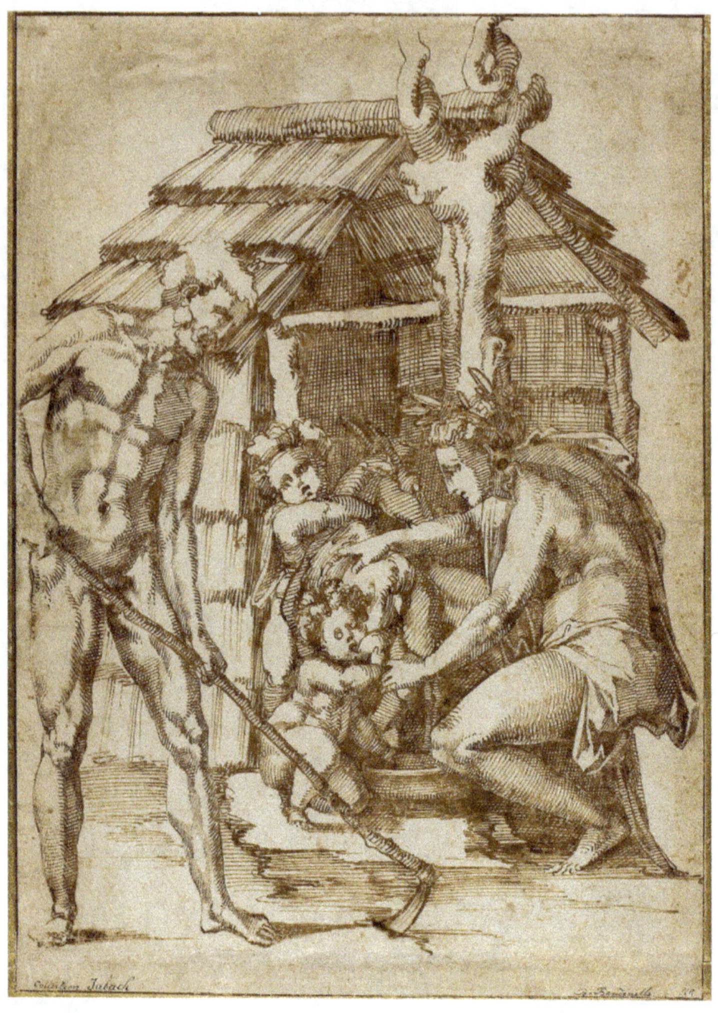

After the fall into sin, Adam and Eve have to make their own way in the world, growing their own food, feeding themselves and their young children as they mature. I wonder, do the children comprehend that they are now mortal, that they are destined to die? They have never seen a person die. What must it have been like to be cast out of paradise, to learn how to survive by scratching out an existence devoid of God's companionship and the endless bounty of paradise? Does this family remember their lives beforehand, or has it all faded like a dream?

We have been given free will, so the possibility to seek out God and his way of life for us is just one of a seemingly endless array of choices we must make. What situations cause us to turn to God for our way of life? Do we, like Adam and Eve, first have to be completely cast out or cast down in order to turn to God? Every reader here has their own story of what it took for them to rely on God in their lives. Sometimes our stories can inspire and lift up others along their way. Let us hope we can do that and that others will do the same for us when we need it most. In the meantime, the cares and requirements of daily living can seem to fill the whole day, leaving little time for devotions and prayer. My hope is that each of us will find time to remember to thank God for our very existence.

PRAYER

Dear Lord, we now live so far removed from paradise that we have to read about it and look at paintings of it to begin to know what it may have been like. In the work-a-day world it is very easy for us to lose sight of our need for you, for the paradise that comes through resting in your peace. The temptation to think that we are in charge and know all of what is best for us, and for others with whom we work and live, is very strong. We fail so often to do the best we can, and, sadly, we do not turn to you unless life has become just too difficult to manage. We thank you for loving us and always accepting us back into your fold. We pray to be worthy of your patience, love, and guidance through the Holy Spirit. Amen.

Head of the Virgin Mary **by Elisabetta Sirani**

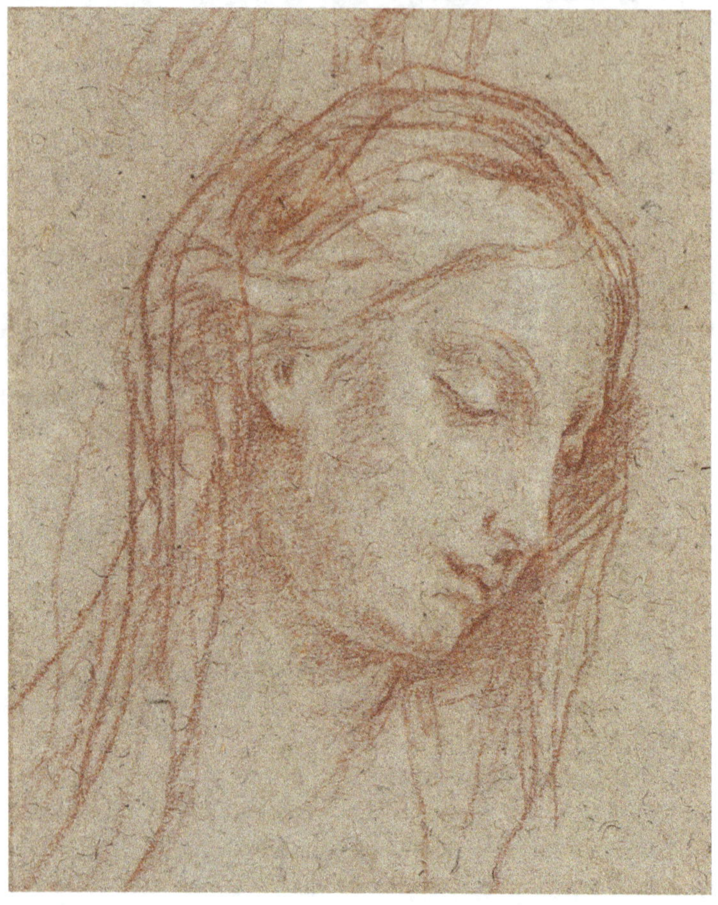

As she gazes down to her right, Mary may be wondering, "How has this happened to me? Will all be well, or should I be worried about what is to come? Shall I trust what this angel has told me?"

When we find ourselves in confusing, even confounding circumstances, do we think first of turning to God, of relying on God's mercy? Or, are we more likely to seek some tangible form of comfort like food, excess activity, or zoning out with Netflix? Let's think about what it is that Mary said in Luke 1:38: "Be it unto me according to your word."

Mary showed complete acceptance based on fundamental trust. Are we capable of such trust when we receive shocking news that could unravel our lives? Most likely not, which is why Mary's response is so exceptional. Her trust in God's plan for her, her absolute acceptance of God's will, sets a supreme example for all of us. Mary can be the model we try to emulate as we face life's challenges. Of course, we will have none that match the one that God gave Mary! Her challenge lasted from becoming inexplicably pregnant as a young Jewish woman, through the agony of seeing her son crucified and beyond. After witnessing his death and, on the third morning, his resurrection as a corporal being, she had to endure still further, extraordinary events in order to follow her own calling into old age.

PRAYER

Holy God, we know that you are with us throughout our lives. As we face both ordinary challenges and larger ones, including our own eventual demise, help us to remember your grace and endless love for us, even when our problems are largely of our own making. Help us to pray for acceptance and also for the strength to act as needed for your sake and our own. We believe you can deliver us from distress when we turn to you. In Jesus' name we pray. Amen.

Joseph Greeting His Brothers **by Pier Francesco Mola**

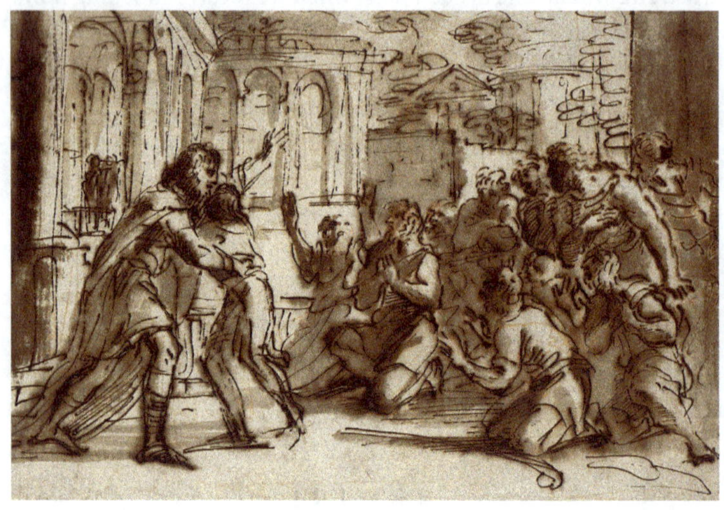

Here we see the unexpected, seemingly-impossible return of a man whom his brothers assumed was forever lost if not dead. How overwhelming for all concerned to see Joseph alive and well. The first brother to greet him is Benjamin, who was blameless in the sale of his brother into slavery. We imagine that each older brothers' reaction must be a variation on the theme of "how can I explain or excuse my role in Joseph's disappearance?!" Each brother is well aware of his own culpability in letting Joseph be sold into slavery.

Have you ever had role that you "had to" or chose to play in an event that was dastardly? Each of us have likely been betrayed, or perhaps we have also betrayed others who trusted us. It is likely that both kinds of experience have occurred multiple times for you.

Although it may be painful, when we reflect on this powerful drawing, we are compelled to recall our own past actions. How and when did we betray someone or get rid of evidence of such choices? What did we learn about ourselves by conspiring against someone for our own benefit? Or out of jealousy? Can God's presence in our lives help us to examine our motivations in the future in order to change the actions we then take? There are many lessons we can learn about ourselves, and our innermost motivations by paying attention to the story of Joseph. Let us take this opportunity to do so.

PRAYER

Dear Lord Jesus, we know that jealousy is a base emotion that any of us can feel, as small children and as mature adults. Please help us remember that you love all of us more even than we can imagine. Your love is like the kind of love we experience for a precious, vulnerable infant. Further, Lord, help us realize that you can enable us to accept these jealous feelings without having to act on them to the detriment of others, whom you also love! Steady our hearts, as we pray that we can rest in you, ignoring the impulse to act in jealousy. Help us to know we are safe and that you love each of us abundantly, with all of our human frailties and our unique ways of being. Guide us and keep us when we face the temptation to get rid of a problem through actions that will eventually cause harm to all concerned. Amen.

Saint Peter Liberated from Prison **by Baccio Bandinelli**

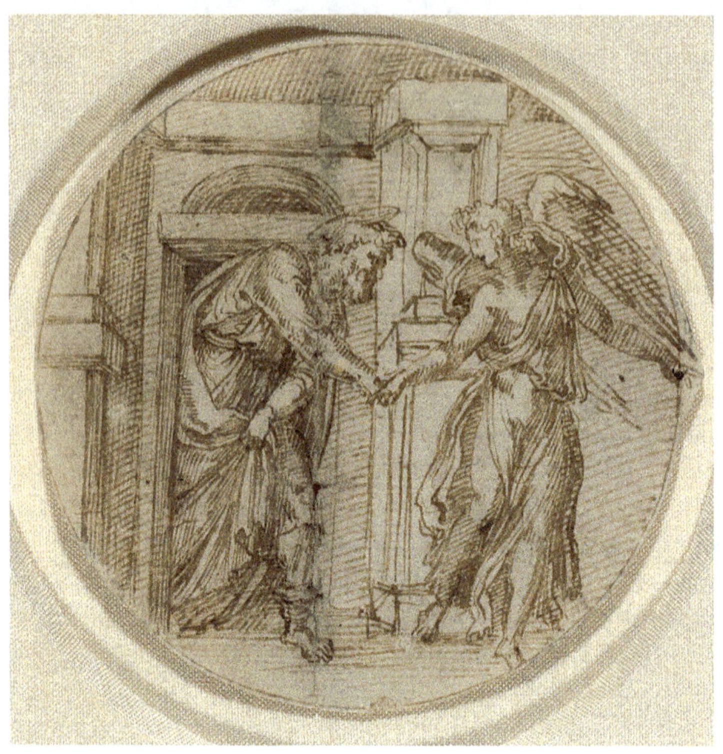

This is a wonderful subject portrayed here in miniature form. In the biblical story found in Acts 12:5–17, Peter is languishing in prison when an angel appears by his side to liberate him. We can imagine Peter, deprived of light, fresh air, and healthy food, becoming very confused by this change in his circumstances. Perhaps he cannot quite believe his own eyes! The angel causes the guards to fall asleep, the chains to fall from Peter's hands, and the doors and gates swing open. He then extends his hand to Peter. God has other plans for Peter than to allow him to be locked up!

In what ways do we feel ourselves to be imprisoned? Is it due to wants and addictions? Have we had bad experiences that we cannot forgive or forget? Are we imprisoned by ill health or the actions of others, including the actions of family members? Above all, are we imprisoned by our own actions and decisions? Whether our imprisonment is of our own making or circumstances beyond our control, we are stuck dealing with the situation. The only way out of imprisonment is to go through whatever it takes to get to the other side. And sometimes—as in the case of illness or disability—that isn't possible.

For most of us, God will not send an angel to free us, but he can help us cope with whatever life brings our way. God can show us what we have to accept and what we can change. We note that in this same biblical story James was also imprisoned, like Peter, but James was executed (12:2) while Peter is freed by an angel so he can continue his calling. He can give us the faith and strength to make the decisions or changes that are needed, and that will bring our lives more in alignment with God's will for us. God alone can also give us the power to accept those things that cannot be changed.

PRAYER

We thank you, Lord Jesus, for your mercy and compassion. We ask that you help us to listen and rely on you as our source of strength and salvation. Humble us, Lord, to understand that, whatever may be the cause of our imprisonment, you will always help us cope with the circumstances. We remember that you told us, "Come to me, all you who are weary and burdened and I will give you rest. Take my yoke upon you and learn from me. . . . For my yoke is easy and my burden is light" (Matthew 11:28–30). Help us Lord to come to you and to stay by you. Remain in our hearts, we pray. Amen.

Saint Ambrose Baptizing Saint Augustine by Ciro Ferri

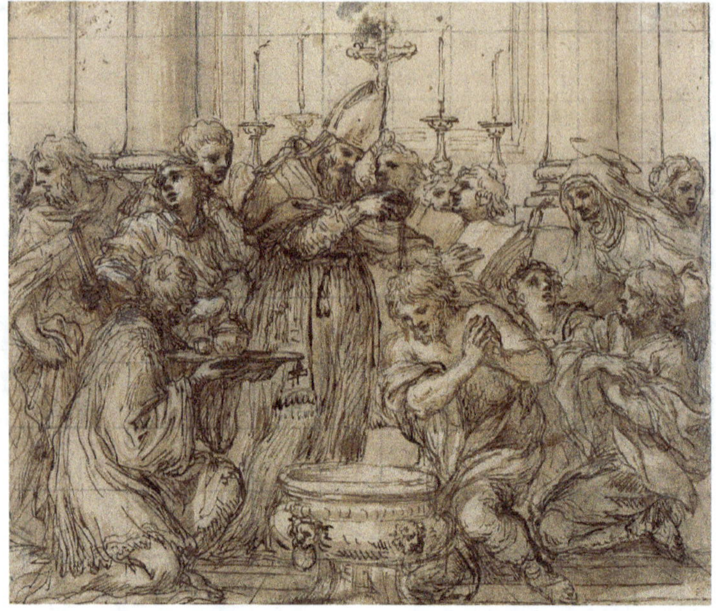

In this elaborate drawing, we see Augustine, simply clad, kneeling faithfully, while he is baptized by Ambrose, the Bishop of Milan. This depicts a historical event that took place in 387 AD. Augustine smiles expectantly, his eyes cast downwards. Still, his pose is dynamic. One can picture him jumping up to his feet at any moment. Subsequently, Augustine became an influential leader of the early church—indeed, a bishop, following in Ambrose's footsteps. He wrote and taught on numerous aspects of theology throughout his life. His legacy helped to shape Christian doctrine for many centuries, and it still influences scholars and the faithful today. He was subsequently declared a saint and is one of only four "doctors" of the church. But in the image before us we see only excitement. One can almost hear the voices of the people observing and participating as they are talking and exclaiming over what they are witnessing. Everyone appears to be in motion in this happy, active scene. Witness especially his mother, Monica (the woman with the halo). She had prayed for many years for her wayward son to come to Christian faith, and now, at long last, he had!

Baptism is such an integral part of becoming a Christian. In my tradition, most baptisms are given to infants, so there is something special in choosing to be baptized as an adult. It must demand a full participation in faith to submit to the baptismal rites as an adult in front of the whole congregation. Who among us willingly and humbly submits to having water poured over one's head like that? Yet it is also a cause for true celebration! At the conclusion of the baptism portion of the service, we say, "We welcome you into the household of God, confess the faith of Christ crucified, and share with us in his eternal priesthood." Now that is something to celebrate! Imagine choosing to receive this Sacrament while in the presence of your friends and family. God knows that by this choice the person being baptized is showing they sincerely want to be close to him and to be a more active part of a faith community. How exciting it that? No wonder Augustine looks so happy.

PRAYER

Dear Lord, whether we were baptized as little ones, in childhood, or as adults, we ask that you help us to continue to celebrate the sacrament that brings part of your domain here on earth. We have chosen you, just as you have made yourself available to us. Guide us along the way to participate in your eternal priesthood in the here and now, to serve you and our companions on our journey. Amen.

Saint Peter Liberated from Prison by an Angel **by Knupfer**

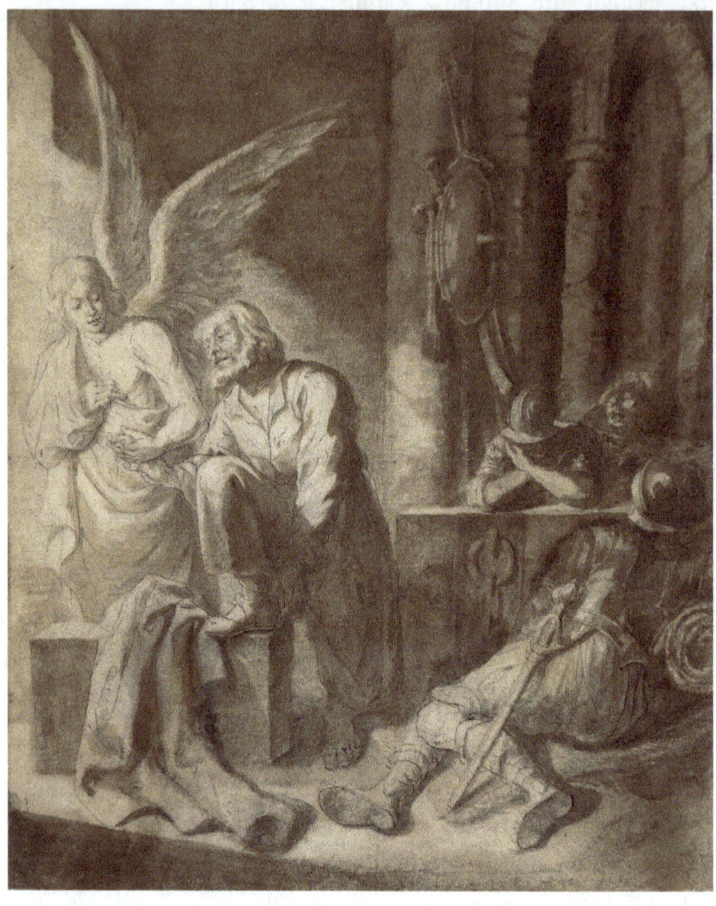

In this large, beautiful, brown ink wash drawing, Peter is awoken by an angel and is blinded by its eminence. Leading up to that moment, Peter has been held in prison. In Acts 12, we are told that the angel instructs Peter to put on his shoes and get his cloak. Peter thinks he must be experiencing a vision, and who in his circumstances wouldn't believe the same? The guards fall inexplicably asleep, and the radiant angel takes Peter out of prison, into the streets of Jerusalem. In the drawing, the angel and Peter both look very peaceful and seem to take their time. The angel's urgency in the Acts narrative is toned down here. Nonetheless, this portrayal of the incident has an appeal all its own. There is a gentleness here that may be very soothing to the viewer. When Peter comes back to his senses, he realizes that what occurred was real.

Most of us will never be imprisoned, waiting to be executed the next morning. But surely there are times when we wish an angel could liberate us from the ways we feel imprisoned by our life circumstances. In the absence of a miracle, how can we rely on our faith to bring us through the darkness we are in? In *Life and Death in Shanghai* by Cheng Nien, the author recounts how she is in prison for her intellectual stance against the Chinese government. There she discovers that although she is physically confined without any basic comforts, no one can imprison her mind. She is free to think as she chooses and to exercise her intelligence unimpeded by the cares and tasks of daily life. Further, no guards can observe the workings of her mind, endangering her further. Therein Cheng finds true freedom.

When Peter returns to Mary's home in Jerusalem as a free man, he relays his experience to those there. Peter tells those gathered to tell James, the brother of Jesus, what has transpired. How can we rely on the practice of our faith to bring light into the places where we are imprisoned in our lives? What resources might we call on to free ourselves mentally if we cannot get free of physical restraints? We cannot think our way out of a handicap or a physical ailment, but we can develop our faith enough to give us a positive perspective on our challenges. This is an ongoing daily practice that is advocated by Thich Naht Hahn amongst generations of faithful Buddhists.

PRAYER

Dear Jesus, you were held captive, scorned, and beaten. You held absolutely firm to your faith. Teach us how to rely on our faith and on you, when we are imprisoned in mind, body, or spirit. Bring light into our darkness. Reveal to us the capacities we have to overcome our own imprisonment. We pray all of this in your name. Amen.

Saint John the Baptist, Kneeling, Raising His Baptismal Cup in His Right Hand **by Palma Giovane**

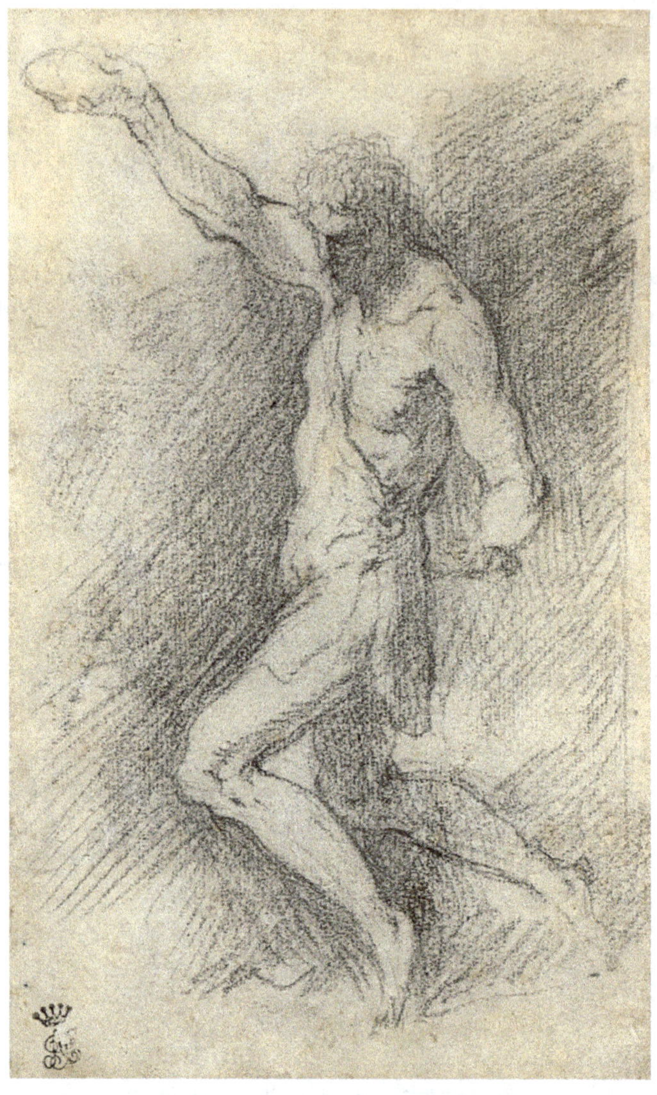

Saint John balances against an unseen boulder as he raises a cup or shell to baptize someone—let us presume it is Jesus. The baptism of Christ presages a brief but significant change of pace in our Lord's life journey, when he leaves to spend forty days of disciplined isolation and meditation in the desert. The event depicted in this drawing comes just as John is baptizing Jesus. God proclaims that Jesus is his beloved Son, with whom he is well pleased. What a positive affirmation of Jesus' prior actions and a blessing for the next phase of his development.

We can only imagine the dynamic energy that flowed between John the Baptist and our Lord when they met as grown men on that riverside! John is the subject of this drawing; we know that he is baptizing Jesus, but we can only imagine that part of the event as Jesus himself is not pictured. Is John the focus because he is more like us than Jesus? John's singular role may be one we can see ourselves in, whereas being the Son of God is completely beyond our ken. We can be inspired by John's humility, reflected in his posture, as he is blessed by participating in this important moment in each of their lives. Do you not wish you had been there? We can understand why John thought that Jesus should be baptizing him, not the other way around. Yet Jesus persuades John to baptize him, according to the Gospel of Matthew, "to fulfill all righteousness." How humble John must have felt at that moment. In the drawing we see that John's head is bent down in a gesture of prayer and perhaps worship. This is the man who proclaimed earlier that "the one who comes after me will baptize you with fire and the Holy Spirit!" What a life-changing experience for all who were witnesses down by the riverside that day.

PRAYER

Dear Lord, when we think of your baptism and the power that was released by you, we may long to have been there ourselves. As we imagine that event, help us to live fully into our own baptisms, to carry out our own ministries by relying on your strength and direction for each of us. This we pray in your name. Amen.

The Annunciation of the Virgin **by Camillo Boccaccino**

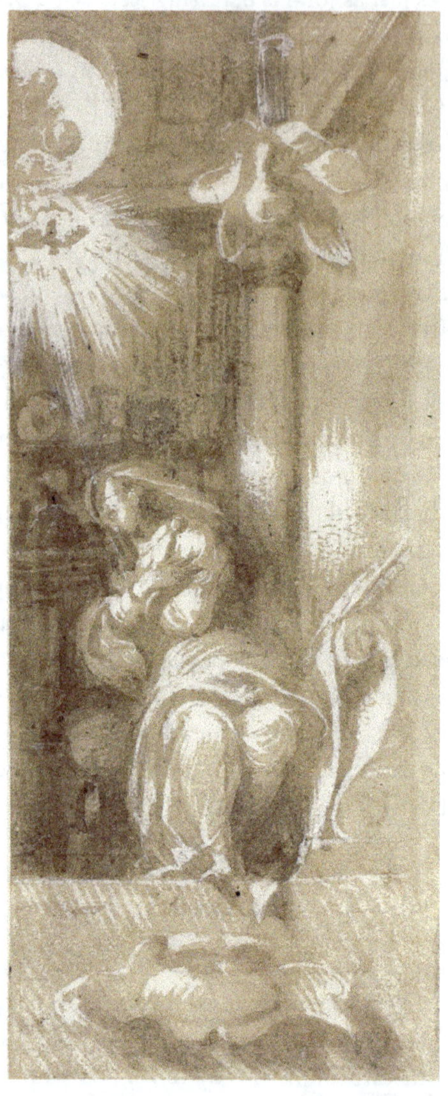

The virgin is leaning to her right in a gesture of humble prayer as she is visited from above by the Holy Spirit and God the Father. She is portrayed sitting in a room with shelves and columns behind her. It is a rather grand setting, and one might wonder what has brought a humble girl to such a place.

Mary does not appear frightened or surprised, and she bows her head in acceptance of what she is hearing. In works of art that illustrate this passage from the Bible, we most often see an angel delivering this singular message to Mary. It is significant that both God the Father and the Holy Spirit are the messengers in this drawing. Perhaps that is why the room is a grand one.

We are told that Mary's response to the annunciation is to say, "I am the Lord's servant, may your word to me be fulfilled" (Luke 1:38). Then the angel leaves her. How does a girl aged fifteen or so cope with such a statement concerning her own future? Christians and art historians are so familiar with images of the annunciation that we may not consider how very powerful that experience must have been for young Mary. Is it through God's grace that she is able to be so calm and accepting of such incomprehensible news?

PRAYER

Dear Lord, while our lives may be filled with surprises, we will never experience a revelation like the one you gave to Mary. Yet we need to rely on something when we are shocked by news or the turn of events in our lives. Lord, let it be you to whom we turn when we are overwhelmed by news or events. We know that we cannot manage on our own, but we need your help to manage the stormy seas of life. Come to our aid we pray. Amen.

The Deposition by Ferrau Fenzoni

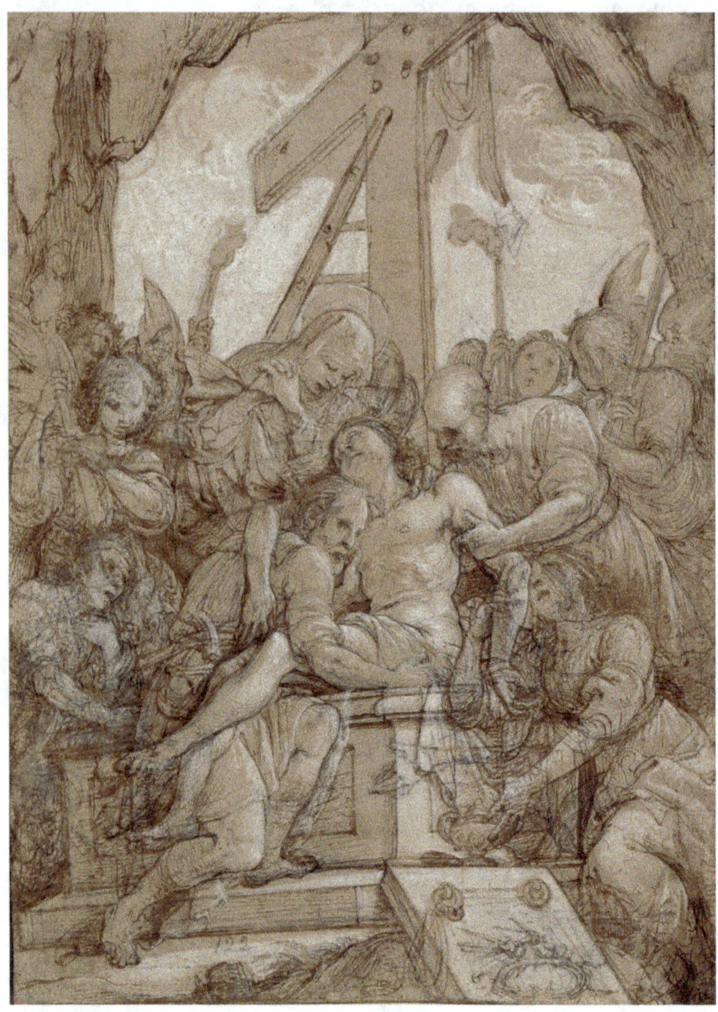

In this dynamic drawing, Fenzoni used many media, pen and brown ink over black chalk, underdrawing, and brown ink wash, heightened with lead white gouache on brown laid paper. This drawing is preparatory for a large painting Fenzoni made for his own funerary chapel in Faenza. The painting would have gone above the altar in that chapel. Thus, we can imagine how well Fenzoni liked this subject and how hard he must have worked on its composition. It is a complex piece. Many of the figures appear to be in motion. We can identify the two men laying Jesus in the tomb as Joseph of Arimathea and Nicodemus. We also see the virgin standing above and to the left of Jesus, and Mary Magdalene is kneeling below, to his right, with another woman kneeling to his left. It is dark in the cave where this tomb is located. There are four torches, two held by angels and two by others present.

You will note that the Magdalene's head and left arm are drawn in two different positions. This *pentimenti* indicates that Fenzoni is experimenting to see what each head and arm position looks like to determine which position he will employ in his final work. Notice also that Mary Magdalene has a delicate halo over her head indicated with faint white gouache. What do you make of her expression as she gazes upwards? With the right arm in the bent elbow position, she may be wiping away a tear. We cannot know, we can only perceive, and each of us will perceive it differently.

This image is engaging at many levels. The sheet is completely finished, with the lines drawn on the upper edges indicating the shape of the cave in which the tomb is placed. Again, virtually every figure is in motion, reacting to the drama of Jesus' death and the terrible beauty of his limp figure. Here we see each of these people reacting to the moment when Christ is laid in the tomb. The caring expression of the man supporting Jesus' left shoulder is especially moving. The man with his right forearm supporting Jesus' left thigh and hip is looking directly at the viewer! Notice that there is a hammer in his belt, so he must have climbed up to free Jesus' limbs from the cross! What must that have felt like for this man who is gazing directly at us? Consider the placement of this figure. He is placed very near the center section of the drawing. This scene is crowded with figures, some only indicated by a partial view of their faces. I find the facial expression of the angel at the left center edge particularly subtle and moving.

Perhaps you have not seen many images of the deposition of Jesus. For Christians such pictures are usually deeply moving, and as we see in comparing this drawing to *The Deposition* by

Poliodoro, also in this volume, they vary widely in how the event is portrayed.

We may have plans for our own burial, but I suspect we do not picture our own dead bodies or who will handle them, preparing them for the coffin or funereal urn. As stated in the Poliodoro da Caravaggio meditation, we in the US do not handle our own dead loved ones to prepare them for burial, as was the case until earlier in the twentieth century. I consider this to be a loss for us, for we no longer get to lovingly care for the body of our loved one before it is laid to rest. It could be so comforting to prepare the remains for their final resting place, an act of love and of hope in the resurrection! That brings us back to the image we contemplate here; there is a huge group participating in this final act of love and respect.

PRAYER

Father, artworks of the entombment of your blessed Son help us imagine more fully what his traumatic sentence and death meant to his followers. We see in works like the one pictured above that his followers were totally bereft, thinking that his death was the end of the story. As we view such works of art, while we can share in their sorrow, we can also be eternally grateful for his death because we are saved through his resurrection three days later. On Easter the Son will rise from the dead with the gift of eternal life for us all. Help us to never take his sacrifice for granted and to hold fast to the hope that this act in which Jesus surrendered his life ensures for each of us eternal life forevermore. Amen.

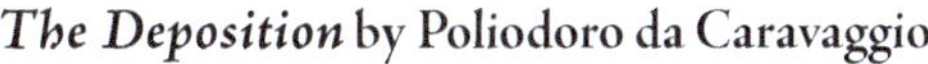

The Deposition by Poliodoro da Caravaggio

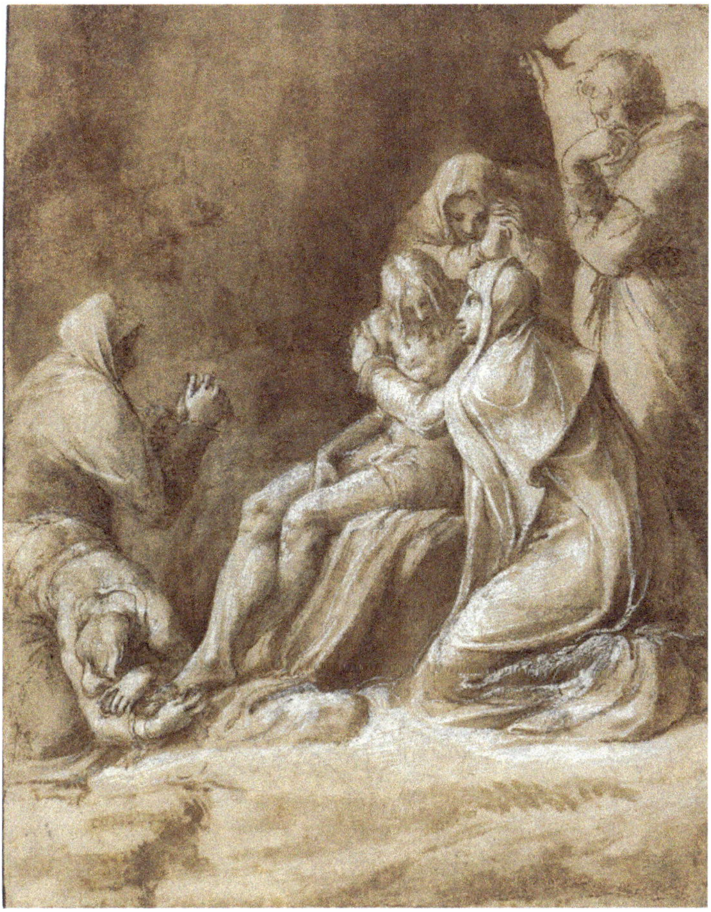

In this somber and moving drawing, we see the body of Jesus being laid down in a cave. There are four women attending him and one man standing at the entrance. Today, we do not get to handle our dead in most cases, so we miss both the deep sadness and also the intimacy that comes from handling the body of a departed loved one. In this image we see that two of the women are praying, while his mother holds him close. The fourth woman, presumably Mary of Bethany, washes Jesus' feet, perhaps with tears of grief this time instead of costly perfume. The darkness of the cave seems cool and provides a protected place to be laid to rest. The man at the opening of the cave looks very pensive, even guarded, as he stands there alone, his hand encompassing his jaw. He appears deep in thought and withdrawn from the corpse and the women tending it.

As Christians steeped in the Gospel story, we can imagine and foresee the women's surprise and horror to find Jesus' body missing, early on Sunday morning, when they come to the cave to attend it, as was customary. The body is the sole precious remainder of their Lord, so it is very dear to them. Jesus had no possessions to leave behind, which might have provided some small comfort for his followers.

Today we know that, thanks to Jesus' crucifixion and resurrection, we have hope when it is our turn to encounter death, knowing that it is not the final chapter of our lives. The cold dark of the tomb that we see in this drawing only *appears* to be the end of the story. Laying Jesus to rest is sorrowful, and it must have been a pain beyond words for those who loved and followed him. As we gaze on this image, we have the benefit of knowing that he will not remain there past the dawn of the third day.

PRAYER

Dear Lord Jesus, we are most grateful to you for willingly giving up your life for us. When we encounter the death of a loved one, we remember that there is more to the story than the cold dead body we can touch and see. We will certainly grieve the loss of that person's company, but we believe that they will become whole and well again as they come home to you. The tomb is just an earthly resting place, not the person's final destination. For this we are grateful beyond what words can convey. Show us how to extend sustained compassion for those who are suffering the loss of a loved one. Teach us to be patient with mourning, in others and in ourselves. Amen.

The Flagellation of Christ **by Master of The Ghislieri Apse**

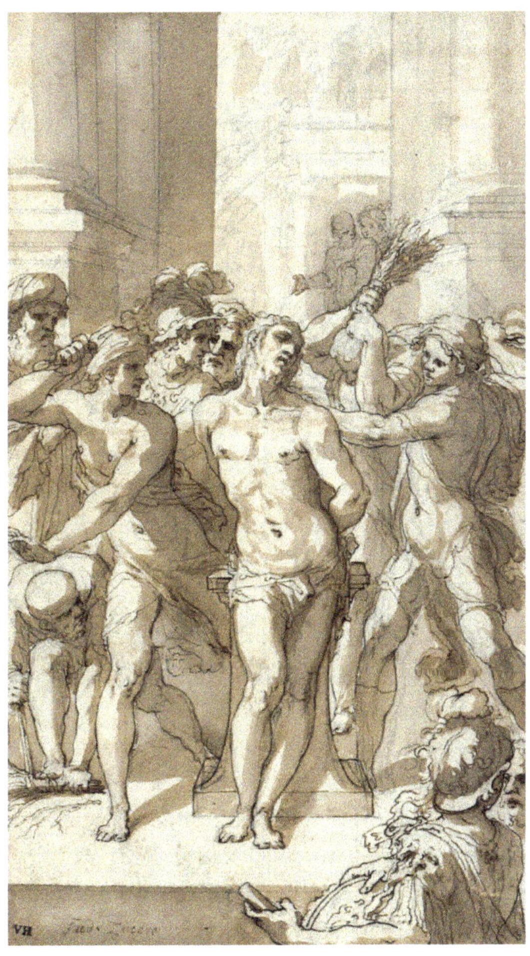

In this beautifully rendered drawing we see Jesus, bound and only covered by a loin cloth, being beaten with flails made of branches and twigs. He appears calm and accepting, perhaps even resigned to this fate. Jesus told his followers that he was going to be given into the hands of sinners to be killed. While this may explain his lack of reaction in the drawing, probably none of us can imagine being forced to submit to the pain and public humiliation of such a beating with any equanimity. Indeed, only the true Son of God could be at peace at such a time.

What does it take to accept such an injustice done to us? How might we cope? Could we remain calm and what alternative would we have? Jesus is bound, helpless, and completely alone. He has been abandoned by those closest to him. There is no earthly possibility of being rescued. To endure such an experience is hard to comprehend.

During Holy Week each year, we have the opportunity to relive Christ's passion history. Sometimes that is a pain-filled experience that we can barely endure. We may feel ashamed of the way Jesus was treated and our shared human part in that mistreatment. It may be that our denial of a bad association or a bad deed is frequently just below the surface in each one of us, as it was for the disciples. Further, we have to re-live the injustice done and the extreme pain inflicted on our Lord, who we strive to love with all our hearts and minds. Had we been there, we too would have been helpless to stop the crucifixion. Then we are confronted with Peter's three denials of Jesus. We ask ourselves, would I have done the same thing to save my own skin? Pain abounds in every aspect of this passion story.

Returning to the drawing, we see two pairs of figures, one in the background behind the flagellation scene, one in the immediate lower right-hand foreground below it, each calmly discussing what they are observing from a distance. Who would they have been? Could we, who know the whole story, imagine simply observing the beating of this innocent man? Have we ever been party to an injustice where we detached ourselves, as these men have done? What kind of internal defense mechanisms are they relying on? Are we ourselves capable of such a cool and indifferent stance?

In the drawing, Jesus alone is still, calm, and seemingly unaffected by what is being done to him. How can we align ourselves with this humble God and man, even though we know he will be raised from the dead in three days? What role would we have played that day, if we had been alive and present then? How can we remember the passion and grow beyond that imagined role? Can we feel the pain of it all and yet come to a place, through God's love, where Jesus' understanding and forgiveness shines through our hearts? What, finally, is the connection between Jesus' tortuous death and our own attempts to live our lives faithful to his teachings and desires for us?

PRAYER

Dear God, when we remember what was done to your Son, our Lord, we are overwhelmed by the horror of those actions. Please forgive us as the descendants of those who abandoned and crucified him. Strengthen us when we deny our own guilt or hide from our part in injustice in our daily lives. Help us to accept the forgiveness of Jesus, who loves us despite all of our human frailties. Show us how to take his love and use it for good in our daily interactions with others. All this we pray in Jesus' name. Amen.

The Incredulity of Thomas by G. B. Castello

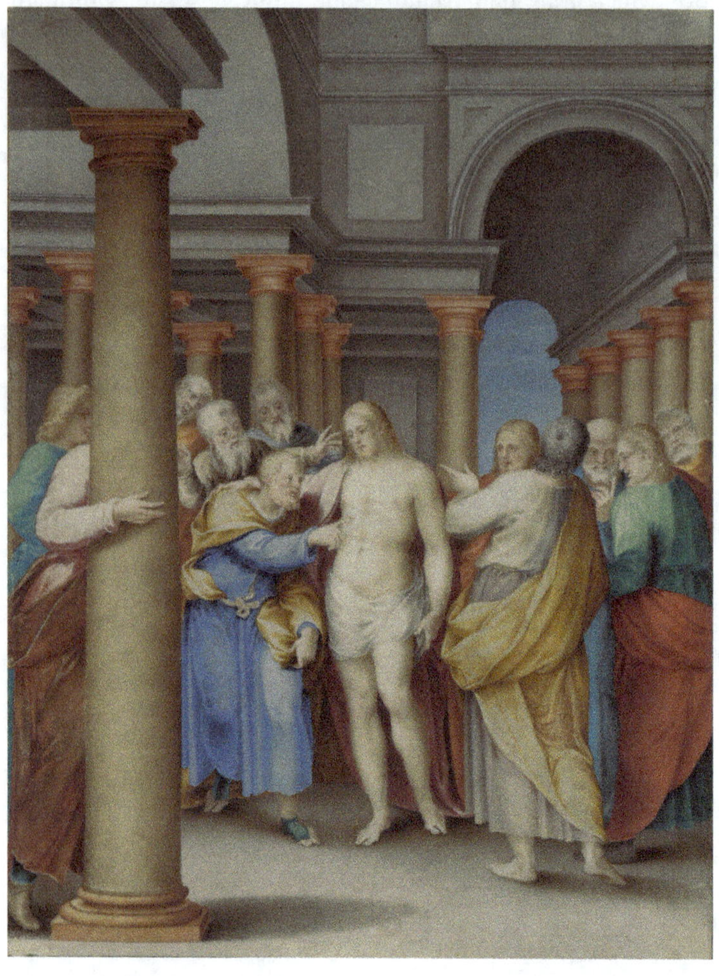

In this colorful image we see the eleven remaining disciples gathered in excitement as they surround the resurrected Jesus. Imagine their surprise at seeing him again! In the gouache image, Thomas is shown tentatively reaching for the open wound in Jesus' side. I am extremely grateful for Thomas and his very concrete sense of what can be true. Perhaps many of you are too. I suspect that all Christians go through periods of doubt. We are just paltry, limited humans after all, trying to grasp the impossible, that Christ was bodily raised from the dead and appeared before his disciples. Not only that, the risen Lord is no mere vision or spirit. He is able to eat and drink like the rest of us. It defies the imagination. What does it all mean? We wonder.

So, Thomas needs concrete physical proof that the man before the disciples is Jesus. Thomas was not with the disciples who first saw Jesus. He said that he wouldn't believe it until he could place his finger in his wounds. When Jesus appears to the disciples through a closed door, he invites Thomas to put out his hand and place it in Jesus' side. Again, we can all share in the gratitude to Thomas for his very human desire for proof of what he had been told. Many of us, young and old alike, need tangible proof of things we've been told. What a relief that one of those in Jesus' inner circle has the same need that we have to see the truth with our own eyes!

There is a curious element in this painting. Have you noticed it? One of the disciples in a dark red robe with pink sleeves is partially hidden behind a pillar in the left foreground. We cannot see his face. Is the disciple leaning against the pillar because he is overcome and needs support? These possible reactions also resonate with me, as I cannot be sure what I might feel if I were one of his disciples upon seeing Jesus again right in front of me. It could well be overwhelming for any one of us. So, I take comfort in seeing this reaction from another of Jesus' followers.

The rest of the disciples are in such serious discussions that they look like a group of academics observing a phenomenon together. What a contrast to the way they all looked just a few days before at the Last Supper.

PRAYER

Lord Jesus, thank you for your miraculous resurrection and return to your followers. We are also grateful that you were so patient and understanding with Thomas, who needed physical proof that you had returned. We ourselves can be just like Thomas in our wish for proof that you exist and that the events of your life story are true. Please Lord, be patient with us in our moments of doubt and show us how to best cope with them as we reach towards you. Through the faith others share with us and through prayer bring us back to a firmer grounding in faith. In your name we pray. Amen.

The Madonna Del Popolo by Federico Barocci

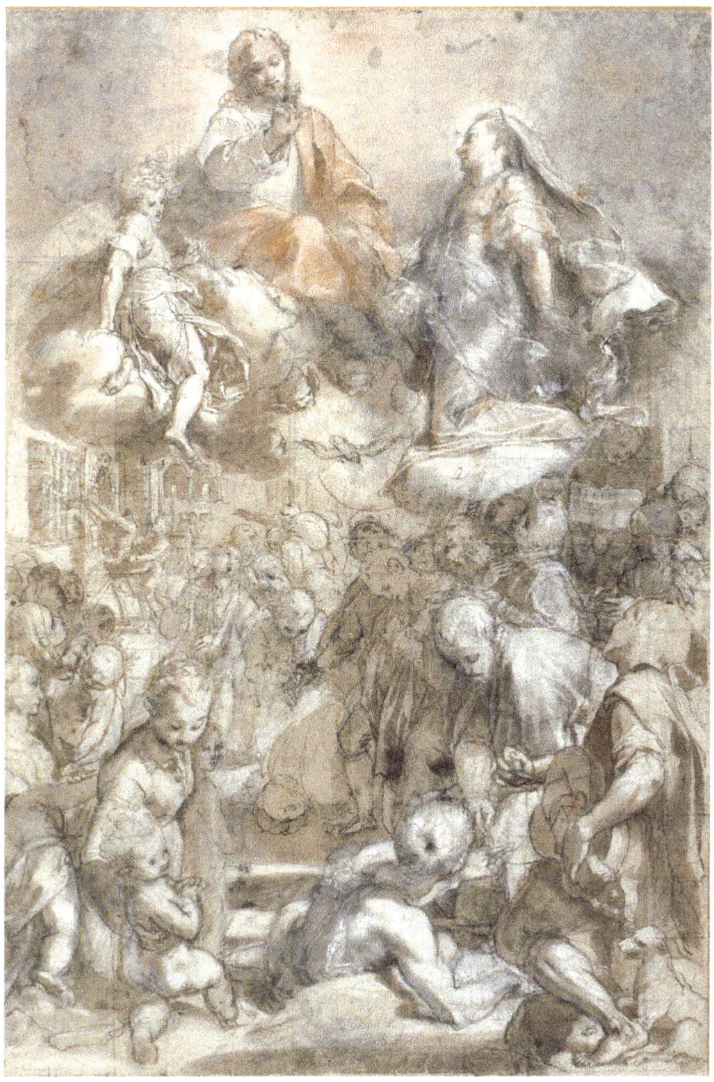

This rich and complex drawing portrays a number of separate scenes, each depicting individuals engaged in the act of giving or receiving charity. Jesus, his mother, and a youthful angel look down from above. The title of this drawing means Holy Mother of the People. We see Mary gesturing downwards as she looks at her son, Jesus, emphasizing the good works that are being done below on the street in his name. The actions being performed in the drawing are referred to as the seven acts of mercy that were given by the members of the confraternity of monks and laymen: clothing the naked; caring for the widows and orphans; caring for the sick and injured; guiding the traveler; and giving food and drink to those in prison. In the lower right quadrant of the sheet, we see a bearded man leaning down towards a reclined figure. We presume that he, as a monk, is going to assist in getting clothing for the mostly naked fellow who is lying in a depression in the path.

The lower half of the drawing is dedicated to human acts of mercy, the upper half to the heavenly host, to Christ in glory, and to the Virgin Mary. Jesus raises his right hand in a gesture of blessing on the scene below. Just underneath the clouds on which they sit, we find the dove that represents the Holy Spirit radiating light as she observes all that is happening below.

It is very reassuring when we extrapolate from the drawing that we have Mary as our intercessor. Let us hope that she also intercedes for us when we are committing sins and selfish acts, not just when we are our best selves performing acts of charity and mercy. In the course of our lives, all of us most probably have been both the caregiver and the care receiver. That cycle is an integral part of how a community functions, as Christian pilgrims know well.

Intercessory prayer is a great gift. We have intercessory prayers for all sorts of situations. It is a comfort to believe that in addition to having intercessors like Mary, we can make a difference for others by faithfully saying prayers for them and their various challenges. We can also learn to ask for prayers for ourselves in times of need.

PRAYER

Dear Lord, most of us want to do good for others, although we rarely follow the rules, unlike the faithful Christians represented in this drawing. It is very easy to focus on our own affairs too much of the time. Guide us, Lord! We pray you help us to accept your life and teaching as our example of right actions. We give thanks and praise for your love and your grace. Amen.

The Return of the Prodigal Son by Lodovicco Caracci

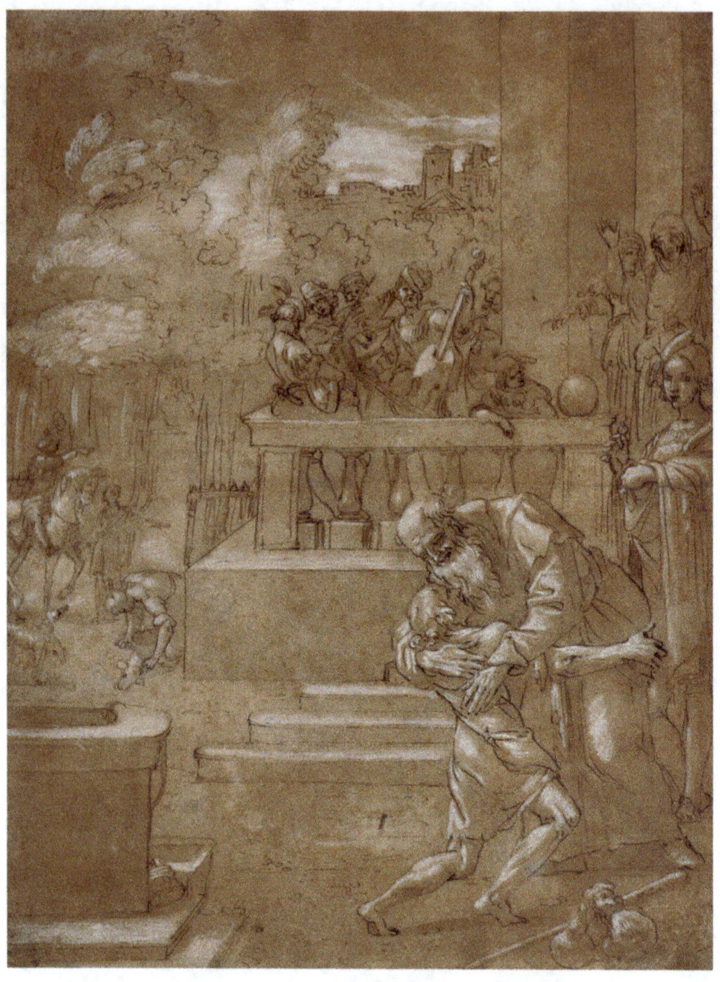

In this fully-developed, brown ink wash drawing there are so many elements in the composition that it may take a moment to realize that it is in the lower right foreground that we see father and son of the title. They are embracing one another. We may imagine tears in the father's eyes as he beholds his dirty and perhaps smelly wayward son. The boy is collapsing into his father's arms, a look of anguish on his face. This is such a famous moment in the Bible that volumes have be written on it. Let's consider what we see here.

Caracci has included all of the parts of the story in a simultaneous rendering in the drawing. The elder responsible son on horseback points to the celebration as if to say, "For whom has a party been assembled?" Even the fatted calf is being slain as onlookers exclaim upon sighting the son in the middle right edge and a servant stands ready above them with the best robe for which the father has called.

Bringing our attention back to the embracing figures, one young and helpless, the older one fully embracing this lost son, they seem oblivious to the activity all around them. This is *their* story. We all hope that if or when we err to a great extent, we can still return to loving acceptance somewhere. Likely, our earthly family and friends will not respond as generously as does the father in the image. They may be quick to judge us and our bad choices. Have you experienced anything like this in your own life?

We may not squander all that we have and eat with the pigs in a trough, but we sure can make a mess of things in our selfish drive to get what we want no matter the cost. We have seen enough actions, our own and others, to recognize the problem in our world. Here we'd best remember that God promises to love us despite all of our failings. In Isaiah 54 we hear, "'The mountains may shift, and the hills may be shaken but my faithful love will not shift from you, and my covenant of peace will not be shaken' says the LORD, the one who pities you." In 1 Chronicles 16:34, we are told that God's faithful love endures forever.

Can we remember to turn to God when we need comfort, acceptance, and forgiveness for what we have done? When our family and friends actively judge us, demanding explanations as they hold on to their anger towards us, we need to call on God to bring us to our senses and maybe to our knees, where we find God's love and the peace that passes all understanding. We can get to this truth of God's abiding love in quiet prayer, in a thoughtful call to God to help us and forgive us. God will not turn away from a request for his help. Great is his faithfulness.

PRAYER

Dear Lord, there are ways in which we are like the prodigal son. We may fall into trouble or seek it out; either way, we mess up, hurting and disappointing our loved ones, time and time again. We know, Father, that you will come to our aid, giving us the grace to be penitent and to ask for your guidance to a better way of being. Your never-ending love will help us turn around and do better. Thank you for always loving us. Amen.

IN CONCLUSION

The Celts talk about "thin places." These are places where the Holy can be felt; heaven meets earth and eternity meets time. They are places where if you just stand still you can feel the reality of God.

It was Barney Hawkins, the pastoral theologian, who suggested that we need to extend the concept of "thin places" to encounters with people.[2] Barney's description of his daughter Ellen—a person with Downs Syndrome—is deeply moving. This relationship has become a thin place wherein Barney encounters God through Ellen's way of being in the world. Where Barney Hawkins wants to extend the concept to human relationships, we wish to extend it to the arts and visual arts. The encounter with great art is a deeply significant moment. It is an encounter with creativity: here is a human life capturing a moment in art; it is an encounter with a distinctive way of looking at the world; unlike a photograph, the artistic rendering is inviting us to see the world more deeply; and it is an encounter with the spiritual; it is spirit that underpins the matter.

In these old master drawings one can see beyond the marks on the paper into the source of creation that we call the Divine. This experience will take a different form for different people. It requires time from the viewer to detect the underlying implications about our human condition that the drawing portrays. Since this is a journey into the spiritual realm, it is difficult to pin it down completely. It is a bit like trying to describe what sunlight is; one can only use similes and metaphors. The experience requires some work, and this work is an important part of the process of engaging with the spiritual.

Appreciating the reality that underpins the material is "work." By this, we mean that it requires some effort. Often, we want our experience "pre-packed" and easy to digest. With the visual arts, one does need to sit with the piece. One needs to linger in a gallery or a museum. One may need to make several visits—and it is only, for example, on the third visit that one notices the two figures

2. See Hawkins, "Finding God in People and Places."

in the background, observing the scene. Then the interpretation will take some time. There is an inevitable sense of variety when it comes to the interpretation. Granted, with a biblical scene the drawing is clearly about that moment in the life of Jesus, but even then, there will be a pluralism of interpretations. Is the drawing exuding calm or anguish? Who is the focus of the drawing?

In chapter 3, we noted how George Steiner, the scholar of English literature, beautifully describes the experience of being engaged with art when he writes: "Entering into us, the painting, the sonata, the poem brings us into reach of our nativity of consciousness. It does so at a depth inaccessible in any other way."[3] Great art goes deep in us. This might be work but it is deeply rewarding work.

Great art and music, created through inspiration, immerses the viewer or the audience in unique images and sound that is wholly an echo of the divine achievement of creating the cosmos out of nothing, as God did. An abstract artist, Makoto Fujimura, postulates the same in his book *Art and Faith*. Fujimura's primary theme is that creativity is the heart of God's work. The drama of creation and of salvation history is a drama of "making." As he puts it: "The Word of God is active, and alive. God the Artist communicates to us first, before God the lecturer."[4] For Fujimura God is the Artist "and this role of God as the Creator/Artist deserves a far more central role in the domain of theology and missions. Therefore, the gospel (as an entire history of God's people) is God's artwork, God's ultimate story."[5] God's creativity is reflected in our creativity as human beings.

Let us, therefore, assume that the "nativity of consciousness" is the beginning or birth of our awareness of ourselves and our ability to perceive, feel, and be creative. Art then brings us back in touch with the elemental perception of beingness, where we can be fully born into our senses. We are suggesting that such experiences bring us to a depth of experience that we cannot achieve without art.

3. Steiner, *Real Presences*, 182.
4. Fujimura, *Art and Faith*, 7.
5. Fujimura, *Art and Faith*, 92.

As Fujimura shows, we are created by God. Therefore, we have the innate gift to create, and as Steiner says, art gives us a depth of experience that we cannot have any other way. We can become more aware of ourselves as created by the Divine Source, who has given us the ability to experience all of this. In addition to contacting the depth of our own being, some of us can create art for others. Great art takes us out of ourselves and makes us aware of the eternal realm and how our experience of art connects us to that realm.

Secularism is real. Increasing numbers of Americans are losing their religious practice. No one has taught them how to pray. No one has shown them how to sit still (disconnected from a device) and allow themselves to sense the divine that surrounds them. The church has made a mistake. The assumption has been that our secular neighbor needs to be "argued" into faith (that God is a lecturer as Fujimura puts it so well). We need to model ourselves on God's interaction with humanity; we need to create something beautiful that becomes a vehicle for showing others the transcendent.

For all these reasons, our plea is that we make the visual arts an aspect of our congregational life. We take for granted that music is a part of worship services. There are so many ways the visual arts can become part of a parish's life. We invite congregational leadership and Christians generally to see the potential in learning from art. Granted the viewer of art needs some training. To appreciate a great painting (or in the case of this book a drawing) takes a guide who can hold your hand and show you the achievement. And this is, in the end, what this book commends. This text can be the guide that enables to reader to view and mediate on great art and see something of God. This is our prayer: this is our hope. We hope that parishioners and clergy will agree and pursue incorporating more visual arts into their liturgy and into the church environment.

Bibliography

Berryman, Jerome W. *Children and the Theologians: Clearing the Way for Grace.* New York: Morehouse, 2009.

Carroll, Noël. *Philosophy of Art: A Contemporary Introduction.* London: Routledge, 1999.

Cartwright, Nancy, and Keith Ward. "The Dethronement of Laws in Science." In *Rethinking Order After the Laws of Nature,* edited by Nancy Cartwright and Keith Ward, 25–52. London: Bloomsbury Academic, 2016.

Davies, Paul. *Cosmic Jackpot: Why Our Universe Is Just Right for Life.* Boston: Houghton Mifflin, 2007.

Farrelly-Hansen, Mimi. *Spirituality and Art Therapy: Living the Connection.* London: Kingsley, 2001.

Fujimura, Mokoto. *Art and Faith: A Theology of Making.* New Haven, CT: Yale University Press, 2020.

Gunn, Giles. "On the Relation between Theology and Art in the Work of Gordon D. Kaufman." *Journal of the American Academy of Religion* 50.1 (1982) 87–91.

Hawkins, Barney. "Finding God in People and Places." In *Experiencing God: Faith Narratives of Episcopalians,* edited by Ian S. Markham and Kimberley E. Dunn, 78–85. Eugene, OR: Cascade, 2024.

Kaufman, Gordon. *An Essay on Theological Method.* Rev. ed. Missoula, MT: Scholars, 1982.

Khalsa, Siri Bhrosa Kaur. "The Highest Meditation." *Sikh Dharma Ministry,* Winter 2017. https://sdministry.org/the-highest-meditation.

Laplace, Pierre-Simon. *A Philosophical Essay on Probabilities.* Translated by Frederick Truscott and Frederick Emory. London: Chapman and Hall, 1902.

Manning, Russell R. "Towards a Critical Reconstruction and Defense of Paul Tillich's Theology of Art." *ARTS* 16.2 (2004) 32–37.

Maritain, Jacques. *Art and Scholasticism.* London: Sheed and Ward, 1930.

Markham, Ian S. *Understanding Christian Doctrine.* 2nd ed. Oxford: Wiley Blackwell, 2017.

Nasr, Seyyed Hossein. *Islamic Art and Spirituality.* Albany: State University of New York Press, 1987.

Polkinghorne, John. *One World: The Interaction of Science and Theology.* London: SPCK, 1986.

Sohn, Hohyun. "Ryu's Pungryu Theology as a Theology of Art: The Trinity of Oneness, Beauty, and Life." 한국기독교신학논총 *The Korean Journal of Christian Studies* 57 (2008) 179–202.

Sotheby's. "Marc Chagall: Dream, Memory, Love, and Life." *Sotheby's*, February 3, 2023. https://www.sothebys.com/en/articles/marc-chagall-dream-memory-love-and-life.

Spretnak, C. *The Spiritual Dynamic in Modern Art: Art History Reconsidered, 1800 to the Present.* New York: Palgrave Macmillan, 2014.

Steiner, George. *Real Presences.* Chicago: University of Chicago, 1989.

Stowell, Steven F. H. *The Spiritual Language of Art: Medieval Christian Themes in Writings on Art of the Italian Renaissance.* Studies in Medieval and Reformation Traditions. Leiden: Brill, 2014.

Tofani, Anna Maria Petrioli. "The Role of Drawing in Italian Art." Paper presented at the Art Institute of Chicago, Chicago, April 4, 2012.

Ward, Keith. *The Battle for the Soul.* London: Hodder and Stoughton, 1985.

Williams, Rowan. *Grace and Necessity: Reflections on Art and Love.* Harrisburg, PA: Morehouse, 2005.

www.ingramcontent.com/pod-product-compliance
Lightning Source LLC
LaVergne TN
LVHW050540100826
845148LV00002B/628

* 9 7 8 1 6 6 6 7 7 5 7 2 3 *